JÄGER & SC

DRESS AND DISTINCTIONS

1910–1914

H. Kinna and D.A. Moss

Bellona Publications
Argus Books Limited,
14 St. James Road,
Watford, Herts

First published 1977

ISBN 0 85242 497 3

Printed and bound in England for Argus Books Ltd
14 St. James Rd., Watford, Herts. by
Eyre & Spottiswoode Ltd, Grosvenor Press, Portsmouth

Contents

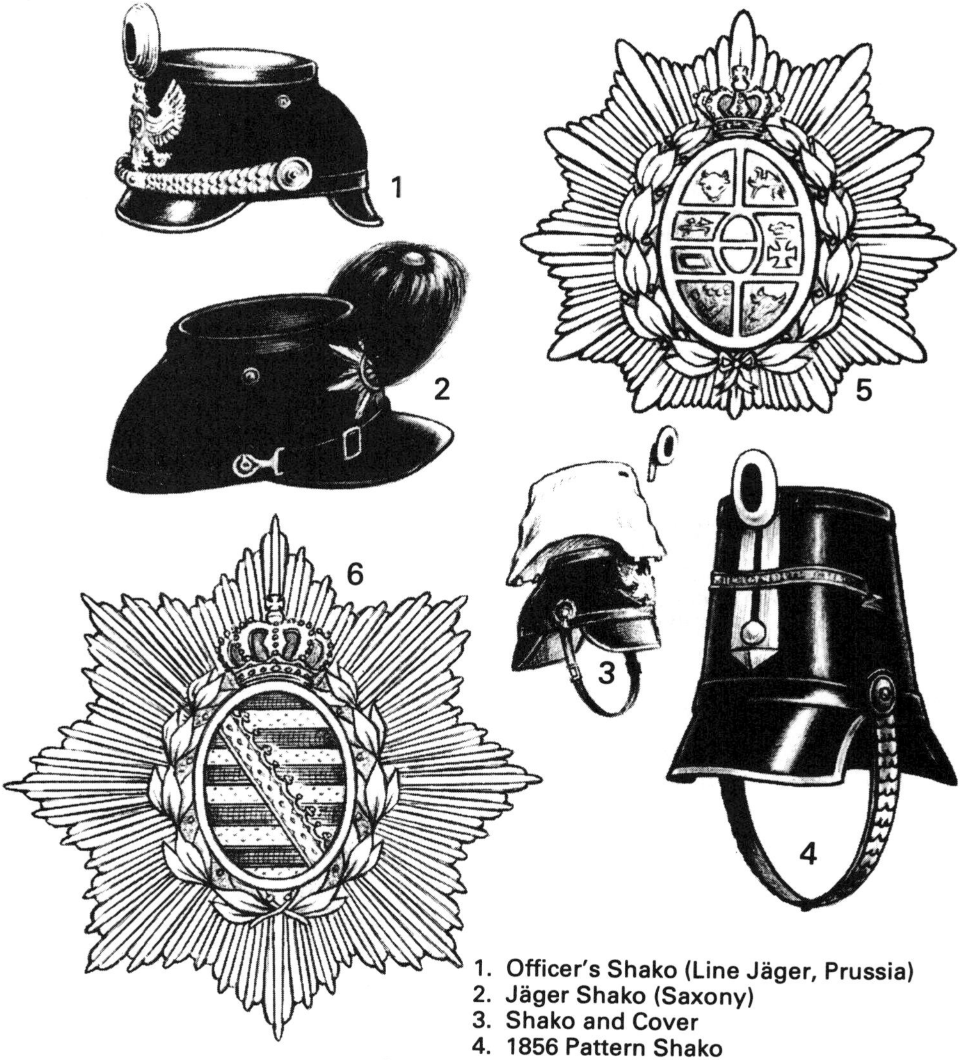

1. Officer's Shako (Line Jäger, Prussia)
2. Jäger Shako (Saxony)
3. Shako and Cover
4. 1856 Pattern Shako
5. Shako Plate (Mecklenberg)
6. Shako Plate (Saxony)

[Notice the great reduction in height of the later Shako.]

Preface

REPRESENTING only a small proportion of the Imperial German Army, the Jäger (hunters) and Schützen (sharpshooters) nevertheless carried a prestige far transcending their actual number. Basically of light infantry character and of an independent and largely volunteer nature, they presented an *élite* image such as the modern paratrooper bears in relation to the orthodox infantry.

Specialising in difficult terrain, often well in advance of the main body, the Jäger excelled in a skirmishing capacity, operating on a more roving and independent basis than the conventional infantryman, and combining all the attributes of the hunter with that close affinity with nature that only the professional forester acquires. The Schützen, on the other hand, originally formed the sharpshooter element of the third or fusilier battalions of the various infantry regiments, frequently utilised in a 'detached' manner but remaining under the wing of their parent formation. In other respects they shared the light infantry character of the Jäger and the qualities of superb marksmanship and expert fieldcraft. This common bond in the course of time was to lead to the title of Jäger identifying both rifleman (hunter) and sharpshooter.

Unique in many ways, the Jäger called his rifle a 'Büchse' (carbine) rather than a 'Gewehr' (rifle); his bayonet he termed 'Hirschfänger' (hunting knife) and he carried instead of the conventional infantry pack a 'Dachs' or badger. (See page 21.) The Jäger also developed a method of communication and manner of terminology peculiar, and often only understandable, to themselves, and alone in the entire army the NCO was entitled 'Oberjäger', the Musician 'Waldhornist', all signals were transmitted by the 'hunting horn', and the final charge often accompanied by the traditional hunting-cry 'Horrido!'

The green-coated Hessians appeared on the military scene as early as 1631, fighting three companies strong on the side of Gustav Adolphus during the Thirty Years' War. Since then most of the German princes raised Jäger formations from their estates, most of a temporary nature but some, particularly those of Hesse, Hanover, Ansbach-Bayreuth and Brunswick, on a more permanent if often mercenary basis, finding their way to the New World there to encounter, perhaps the greatest Jäger of them all, the North American Indian.

Hanover particularly played a great role in the history of both Jäger and Schützen, fighting side by side with, and as part of, the British Army for many years; participating in the Gibraltar Siege; and within the 'King's German Legion' in their 'Schützen' black and green in most of the Napoleonic campaigns – including the Peninsular and Waterloo – culminating in their magnificent defence at La Haye Sainte. Ties remained strong between England and Hanover for many years after this and many Hanoverians remained in the British rifle regiments.

Frederick the Great first placed the Prussian Jäger on a sound military basis with the establishment, about 1744, of the combined Feldjägerkorps, composed of both mounted 'Jäger zu Ross', and dismounted, 'Jäger zu Fuss', regiments, all exclusively drawn from a forestry background. The foot Jäger, together with the Schützen or Sharpshooter units, generally formed a part or the whole of the light battalions of the infantry regiments, and in their 'Zeisig' or finch-green coats with poppy red facings (black in the case of the Schützen), won a renown the length and breadth of Europe.

After the twin disasters of Jena and Auerstedt and the general collapse of the Prussian Army, the remnants of the Jäger Corps and Schützen formations were reformed in 1808; the Jäger as the basis of the Guard and East Prussian Jäger battalions, with Silesia adding an *élite* Schützen battalion composed solely of picked marksmen. In 1814 Prussia added the exclusive Guard Schützen, raised from the former principality of Neuchatel in Switzerland, and a year later the Magdeburg Line Jäger and Rhenish Line Schützen battalions, the former in part derived from the Russo-German Legion and the Saxon Banners ceded to Prussia, the latter from the dissolved Volunteer Jäger detachments and Schützen units from Berg, Nassau and the Saxon light infantry.

From 1821 the Line Jäger and Schützen battalions were each divided into two Abteilungen or Sections, to form four of Jäger and four of Schützen, each two companies strong, with the Jäger Sections integrated within the I–IV Army Corps and the Schützen the V–VIII. Later, in 1845, for tactical reasons, the Schützen, up to this time employed in their traditional Sharpshooter role, were re-entitled Jäger, and from 1848 all sections were increased to three companies and were designated Jäger, battalions 1–8. In 1852 they further adopted a fourth company. The Sharpshooter traditions continued to be upheld by the Guard Schützen and in many subtle ways among the Line Jäger Battalions that had a Schützen origin. In 1866 Jäger Battalion 9 was formed and after the conclusion of the 'Seven Weeks' War' the former Guard and Line Rifles of Hanover became JB10 and the Hessian formations JB11. Throughout the 1870 Campaign the combined Jäger of Prussia, Mecklenburg, Bavaria, Saxony and Württemberg fought with great distinction; Bavaria contributing eight battalions, Saxony and Württemberg each three—the latter dissolved after the cessation of hostilities not to re-appear again until 1914. The 1870 campaign was the last war in which the Jäger and Schützen appeared in their traditional coloured uniform, and in the case of the Bavarians a somewhat closer affinity with the infantry was maintained by their identical sky-blue uniform only differing in its light green facings. The Württembergers also retained this feature, wearing the double-breasted dark blue infantry Waffenrock of the period, but combined with the green facings and shoulder 'wings' of the Jäger rifleman and displaying their individual green 'Schützenschnur' upon the breast.

In peacetime 1914 the Jäger comprised eighteen active battalions; Prussia possessing both the Guard Jäger and Guard Schützen together with the Line Jäger battalions 1–11, Saxony adding 12 and 13, Mecklenburg its former light infantry as 14, and independent Bavaria its own 1st and 2nd Jäger battalions. From 1913 each Jäger battalion adopted an additional Cyclist and MG Company. Saxony also provided the remarkable Regiment No. 108, additionally entitled both Schützen and Fusilier, numbering among the active infantry regiments yet considered of Jäger character while retaining its Schützen identity. All Saxon formations upheld this principle by the retention of black facings as opposed to the red of the Jäger.

In the early stages of the war the Jäger maintained their traditional advanced scouting tactics, often in close co-operation with the cavalry, inflicting 'bee-stings' rather than engaging in heavy pitched battle, but with the stagnation of trench warfare became increasingly committed as normal infantry with most of the more mobile Cyclist units transferred to the Balkan or Eastern areas. During the winter of 1914–15 more specialised units, such as the Württemberg and Bavarian Ski-Jäger, had appeared, closely followed, in May 1915, by the establishment of the German Alpine Corps with its Gebirgs or Mountain Jäger. As the war proceeded the original battalions, reinforced by the Reserve, were reformed into brigades, then regiments, and finally integrated within various infantry divisions. By 1917 specialist Jäger Storm Companies had even appeared, principally with JB3, acting as trench raiding parties, equipped not only with grenades and light machine-guns but also portable trench mortars and flame-throwers, weapons previously the preserve of the Pioneer. By 1918 the Jäger and Schützen were scarcely discernible in tactical employment from the ordinary infantry and only a handful of battalions could still be termed independent.

This book, however, is devoted to describing military uniform rather than organisation, therefore it would be pertinent to mention here why the title dates 1910–14 are given. The last major dress reforms of the peacetime German uniform took place in 1895/96 and, with only very minor subsequent alterations, remained unchanged until 1914. On the other hand the field grey or grey-green manoeuvre dress was not officially adopted until 1910, and represented a completely new uniform devised for the event of war. From this date until the outbreak of war both the peacetime dark green and the field grey or grey-green service dress were worn side by side. Only after mobilisation can the entire army be said to have transformed into field grey. Therefore when speaking of the initial field grey dress, as in Section III, the dates 1910–14 seem apposite (the old-style coloured uniforms being also still in use during this period). The drawings on the back cover, although based on 1900 originals, in fact depict the peacetime uniform as it appeared between 1895–1914.

Finally, though dress, tactics and equipment altered almost beyond recognition, the Jäger spirit of 'first in the field and last to leave' – equally applicable to the Schützen – remained unchanged, and the title Jäger, no matter how prefixed, still remains today a permanent tribute to the memory of the original 'Grasshoppers'. So Riflemen all raise the old cheer 'Vive le Roy et ses Chasseurs!'.

[The illustration on the title page shows a Feldwebel in Litewka JB10 and a Waldhornist JB7 – 1913]

SHAKO PLATES

Line Eagle (Prussia)

Line Eagle (JB11–Prussia)
Guard Star (Prussia)
Coat of Arms (Bavaria)

'Old Genadier 'Eagle (Prussia)

MEN'S BELT BUCKLES

Prussia

Mecklenburg

Saxony

Bavaria

SECTION I

NCOs and Men

1. THE TUNIC (Waffenrock)

Prussia (Guard Jäger, Guard & Jäger Battalions 1–11)
Entitled the Waffenrock or, literally, 'coat of arms', the tunic of the Jäger and Schützen closely paralleled that of the infantry. Traditionally of dark green cloth and fastened by a row of eight buttons, the tunic adopted two vertical arched pocket flaps, one each side of the rear skirt. Each pocket flap displayed three buttons, arranged top, bottom and centre, forming horizontal pairs, the uppermost pair designed as button-hooks to support the belt at the rear.

Piping, 0.2cm wide and of ponceau, or poppy red, cloth, extended the full length of the tunic front, with a similar piping outlining each of the arched tail pocket flaps. The skirt, divided at the rear into individual tails, was provided with inner pockets, the front left-hand serving to contain the field dressings.

The collar, of a semi-stiff stand-up pattern, secured by two pairs of hooks and eyes, was of poppy red cloth for the Guard and Line Jäger and black for the Guard Schützen, piped respectively in light green or red around the front and upper edge. The Guard retained the old square-cut collar, whereas the Line assumed a half-rounded front with, in both cases, a protective black serge neck-cloth appearing just visible above the collar.

Sleeve cuffs of the Jäger were of the Swedish pattern, a simple turn-back poppy red cuff displaying two buttons placed horizontally in line, and for the Guard Schützen of the so-called French pattern, in effect a dark green arched Brandenburg patch, displaying a vertical row of three buttons, mounted at right angles upon the black turn-back cuff. The three outer edges of the patch and the upper cuff were also piped in poppy red. Both cuff patterns possessed a 13cm long seam slit adjustably fastened at the rear by a cloth tab and button.

Shoulder straps were of poppy red cloth and of the Old Prussian pointed pattern displaying, for Line Battalions 1–10, the appropriate number in yellow embroidery, and for JB11 the yellow crowned cipher M (Queen Marguerita of Italy), while the Guard remained without any insignia. Each shoulder strap was secured at the upper end by a small shoulder button embossed with the Arabic number 1–4 for the Rifle, 5 for the MG, or 6 for the 1913-established Cyclist companies. All tunic buttons were of domed yellow metal, in practice an alloy of copper and zinc termed tombac, producing an antique or dark-reddish brass quite distinct from yellow brass. JB10, upholding the traditions of Hanover, displayed a narrow light blue band around the lower right tunic sleeve, 8cm above the cuff, bearing in yellow silk the block-lettered inscription 'GIBRALTAR'.

The Guard was distinguished by a yellow decorative lace of 'Kapellen' pattern upon the collar, assuming a double and elongated form, comprising two rectangular linen bands each terminating at the outer ends in a distinctive chaplet.

Each lace was intersected by a narrow inner light or 'spiegel', with a wider centre dart termed the 'Füllung' formed between the parallel bands. The cuff lace adopted a single and more abbreviated form, upon the Swedish arranged as two vertical laces, and on the French as three horizontal laces, with a single inner light in each case. The display of lace upon the cuff necessitated different button spacing from the customary.

Mecklenburg (Jäger Battalion 14)
The dark green tunic corresponded to the Prussian but retained a square-fronted light green collar piped around the front, upper, and also base edge in poppy red, and light green Swedish cuffs similarly piped red around the upper and rear edge. All tunic buttons were of domed white metal, in practice nickel, and collar and cuff lace was white with light green inner lights. Senior NCOs displayed a woven silver lace. Light green pointed shoulder straps piped around the outer edges in poppy red displayed the red number 14, and poppy red piping extended down the tunic front and around each arched tail pocket flap.

Saxony (Jäger Battalion 12, 13 and Schützen Regiment 108)
Though following the Prussian style the tunic retained certain Saxon characteristics and was of a much darker green, tending to rifle green in shade. The black, half-rounded, collar was piped along the front and upper edge in green and contrasted around the base in red, while the black cuffs piped red around the upper and rear edge were of the so-called 'German' pattern, in effect the Swedish, with a different button arrangement, one button placed on the upper rear cuff, the other vertically in line above, upon the sleeve cloth. In keeping with Saxon custom, the rear pocket flaps were straight, not arched, and each displayed only two domed metal buttons placed top and bottom, the uppermost pair designed in the form of belt support hooks. The shoulder straps were similarly peculiar to Saxony, displaying a square-cut upper end with rounded corners and basically of dark green, piped red around all sides, including an even narrower, about 0.1cm, piping along the base. Upon the shoulder strap was displayed a red battalion number with, placed above, a traditional red hunting horn in cloth not braid. All tunic buttons were of domed pattern and of white metal for the Jäger and yellow metal for the Schützen. The red tunic piping extended down the front and around each tail pocket flap and entirely around the base skirt to terminate at the top of the vertical vent. Unlike the Prussian tunic, which by regulation completely covered the seat, the Saxon skirt was about 8cm shorter and, like that of the cavalry, only half covered the seat.

Bavaria (Jäger Battalion 1, 2)
Conforming to the Prussian pattern the tunic remained traditionally of light blue cloth with a half-rounded light green collar, piped around the front and upper edge in light blue, and light green Swedish cuffs. Light green piping also extended down the tunic front and around each arched tail pocket flap. The pointed shoulder straps were light green with yellow battalion number with all tunic buttons of domed yellow metal.

COLLAR PATCHES [See pages 6 and 7.]

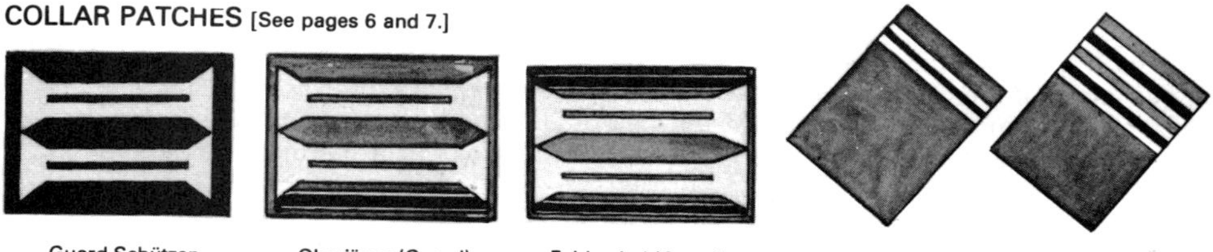

Guard Schützen | Oberjäger (Guard) | Feldwebel (Guard) | Oberjäger (Line) | Feldwebel (Line)

2. RANK INSIGNIA (Dienstgradabzeichen)

Prussia

The Jäger NCO, entitled 'Oberjäger' not Unteroffizier, was primarily distinguished by a golden metallic braid around the front and upper edge of the tunic collar and upon each sleeve cuff. For the Guard the braid was distinctively patterned, whereas that of the Line was completely plain and composed of narrow flat metallic strands. The collar braid, applied in a square-cut manner for the Guard, in the case of the Line smoothly followed the half-rounded contour without any trace of pleat. In both cases a narrow strip of the collar material remained visible between the braid and the outer piping.

Both patterns of cuff braid assumed a square-cut form, outlining the upper and rear edge of the Swedish or, on the French, the upper cuff and front edge of the patch. In both cases a slightly wider strip of the cuff material, about 0.2cm, remained visible above, and in the case of the Swedish to the rear of, the braid. The Feldwebel adopted a second, slightly narrower golden braid ring around each lower tunic sleeve, spaced 0.7cm above the cuff braid.

A more precise indication of rank was the display, on each side of the collar, of either a small, 2.5cm diameter, or a large, 2.9cm diameter, tombac button. The button, not domed, but with a distinctly raised outer rim and embossed with the heraldic Prussian eagle, was positioned directly above and vertically in line with the centre of the shoulder button and tight up to the braid. The Gefreiter, as an advanced soldier or aspirant NCO, adopted the small eagle button upon the collar, the Guard Gefreiter in the same position upon the double lace of the men. Guard NCOs adopted a single yellow collar lace adjoining the rank braid at the front, and upon the Swedish cuff the upper chaplet of each lace was obscured by the rank braid. In 1914 the individual NCO rank insignia were as follows:

(a) Gefreiter (Senior Soldier): On each side of the tunic collar a small eagle button. No collar or cuff braid.

(b) Oberjäger (Corporal): A golden metallic braid, plain for the Line, patterned for the Guard, upon the tunic collar and both sleeve cuffs. No eagle button. NCO without swordknot.

(c) Sergeant (Sergeant): Insignia as Oberjäger, with addition of large eagle button on each side of tunic collar. NCO without swordknot.

(d) Fähnrich (Ensign): Insignia as Oberjäger, but additionally permitted officers' swordknot, officers' topcoat with other ranks' shoulder straps, and officers' head-dress cockade. After satisfactory completion of officers' examination, allowed to carry officers' sword on other ranks' belt. NCO with swordknot.

(e) Vizefeldwebel (Warrant Officer, 2nd Class CSM): Insignia as Sergeant, but additionally carried officers' sword, swordknot and head-dress cockade. Shoulder strap number or monogram of gilt metal as company officer. NCO with swordknot.

(f) Feldwebel (Warrant Officer, 1st Class RSM): Insignia as Vizefeldwebel, with an additional golden braid ring around each lower sleeve. Carried officers' swordknot, sword and head-dress cockade. Shoulder strap number or monogram of gilt metal as company officer. Termed NCO with swordknot. Almost as much an indication of the Feldwebel's status was the brown leather company wallet carried between the unfastened second and third buttons of the tunic, Litewka or greatcoat.

Mecklenburg
Silver patterned collar and cuff braid. Silver heraldic collar button bearing crowned state coat of arms. NCOs from Fähnrich upwards, lace of silver metallic weave, not white linen.

Saxony
(a) Jäger Battalion 12 and 13: Silver collar and cuff braid, plain not patterned. Silver heraldic collar button bearing crowned state coat of arms with lion supporters.
(b) Schützen Regiment 108; NCO termed Unteroffizier: Plain golden collar and cuff braid. Golden heraldic collar button bearing crowned coat of arms with lion supporters.

Bavaria
Golden collar and cuff braid, plain not patterned. Golden heraldic collar button bearing crowned lion rampant, familiarly entitled the 'lion' button.

3. SERVICE GRADE INSIGNIA (Dienststellungsabzeichen)

Prussia
(a) One-year Volunteer: Twisted white/black woollen cord around outer edges of pointed shoulder strap.
(b) Re-enlisted Man: 0.7cm wide white linen band with 0.2cm wide black centre stripe displayed horizontally immediately above the base of the shoulder strap.
(c) Signaller's Badge: Worn on the right upper tunic arm, this displayed two crossed semaphore flags, the one inclined to the left white, the other poppy red, with flagstaffs of lemon yellow, mounted on a circular patch of dark green cloth. Should any other insignia be displayed in this position the badge was transferred to the left upper arm.
(d) Marksmanship School: Those who had satisfactorily completed the course displayed upon the Swedish cuff or French sleeve patch, domed buttons embossed with the heraldic Prussian eagle but without the raised outer rim of the NCOs collar button. The school also awarded its individual silver acorn which, once possessed, superseded the general black/white/red acorns.
(e) Medical Personnel: Displayed on the right upper tunic arm the traditional Aesculapius symbol, in effect a yellow serpent with red eyes and forked tongue entwined around a yellow staff and mounted on an oval patch of dark green cloth. In the field white Red Cross brassard displayed on left upper arm, assistant stretcher-bearers as entirely red brassard.

Mecklenburg
(a) One-year Volunteer: Twisted blue/yellow/carmine woollen cord around outer edges of piped shoulder strap.
(b) Re-enlisted Man: White linen band displaying blue/yellow/carmine centre stripe displayed horizontally across the base of the shoulder strap.

(c) Signaller's Badge: As Prussia.
(d) Marksmanship School: As Prussia.
(e) Medical Personnel: As Prussia.

Saxony
(a) One-year Volunteer: Twisted white/green woollen cord around outer edges of the piped square-ended shoulder strap.
(b) Re-enlisted Man: White linen band with green centre stripe displayed horizontally at the base of the shoulder strap.
(c) Signaller's Badge: As Prussia.
(d) Marksmanship School: Displayed upon the German cuff, buttons embossed with the state coat of arms. These were placed beneath the upper edge of the sleeve cuff in the manner of the Swedish and were additional to the normal two rear buttons.
(e) Medical Personnel: As Prussia.

Bavaria
(a) One-year Volunteer: Twisted white/light blue woollen cord around outer edges of shoulder strap.
(b) Re-enlisted Man: White linen band with light blue centre stripe displayed horizontally at the base of the shoulder strap.
(c) Signaller's Badge: As Prussia but on light blue circular cloth underlay.
(d) Marksmanship School: Cuff buttons embossed with crowned lion rampant.
(e) Medical Personnel: As Prussia except on light blue oval cloth underlay.

4. TROUSERS AND FOOTWEAR (Hosen und Fussbekleidung)

Trousers (Hosen)

Prussia
The cloth service trousers fully corresponded to the infantry pattern and were, since 1870, of an extremely dark blue/black shade, virtually black, displaying on each outer seam a 0.2cm wide poppy red piping. During the winter months, that is from the 1st October to the 30th April, long blue/black trousers were worn with the black laced ankle boots, but with certain orders of dress, cut in the manner of breeches with tapered bottoms and termed 'Stiefelhosen', inside the black leather marching boot. The wearing of the trousers inside the boot, though partly adopted during the 1866 campaign, was not officially sanctioned until 1869.

White linen trousers without piping were worn during the summer months, that is from the 1st May to the 30th September, on such occasions as parade, guard duty, church parade or walking out, always with the black leather ankle boots and not the marching boot. The bottoms of both the cloth and linen trousers were cut to rest in a distinctive inverted 'Vee' manner upon the instep, falling to the rear level with the upper edge of the heel, without the grey leather or white linen retaining strap attached to the base of each trouser leg.

Mecklenburg, Saxony
As Prussia.

Bavaria
Retained traditional light blue cloth trousers with light green outer seam piping.

Footwear (Fussbekleidung)

Prussia
As the infantry, the Jäger utilised two forms of footwear: the high black leather marching boot, the popularly misnamed 'jackboot', with shafts up to 31.5cm high and with studded soles and metal heel protectors, or the black leather ankle boot with plain leather soles and heels. Two forms of ankle boot were worn, one laced at the side adopted 1893, the other at the front introduced 1901, the former termed the 'old', the latter the 'new' pattern. These were carried in the pack when on the march.

Mecklenburg, Saxony and Bavaria
As Prussia

5. GREATCOAT, UNDRESS TUNIC & FATIGUE DRESS (Mantel, Litewka und Drillichanzug)

Greatcoat (Mantel)

Prussia
Conforming to the infantry pattern, the single-breasted greatcoat, officially described as light grey but in reality a much darker medium-grey, fastened at the front by a vertical row of six domed tombac buttons. Sleeve cuffs were of a deep turn-back pattern of the same material as the coat, and a sloping pocket flap without button was situated on each front skirt, the highest points in line with the lowest front button. The back of the greatcoat was plain without pleats, with an attached half-belt at the rear waist secured at the centre by a single domed tombac button, and the divided rear skirt remained plain without ornamental pocket flaps.

The deep collapsible collar was faced each side with rectangular poppy red patches, the Guard Jäger displaying an abbreviated yellow double lace with red inner lights, the Guard Schützen a similar yellow lace upon black patches with black inner lights. For the Line NCOs a 0.7cm wide white linen band with 0.2cm black centre stripe was placed upon the rear of each patch, with a second similar band added for the established Feldwebel. When lace was displayed upon the collar patch, the white linen band was repositioned parallel to and above the upper lace, with the second band of the Feldwebel parallel to and beneath the lower lace.

With the collar raised, retained by a grey cloth tab and button, the Oberjäger was distinguished by a small domed yellow metal coat button placed one each side of the collar band, replaced in the case of the Sergeant, Vizefeldwebel and Feldwebel, by the large eagle button. The Gefreiter, as the men, remained without distinction. The collar when folded, obscured both the upper tip of the shoulder strap and the shoulder button. The shoulder straps, as on the tunic, were of poppy red cloth with yellow number or monogram, or plain for the Guard.

The old dark grey, virtually black, greatcoat of 1867 resembling the cavalry pattern continued to be worn on undress or walking out occasions until stocks were exhausted and was still in evidence in peacetime 1914. This retained the poppy red collar patches and old dark green pointed shoulder straps with red piping and yellow battalion number, for JB11 the yellow crowned monogram M. The Guard retained the red shoulder straps without insignia.

Upon the greatcoat service grade insignia, such as that of the One-year Volunteer or Re-enlisted Man, etc, was retained but sleeve badge insignia and swallows' nests were not adopted.

In the field the greatcoat was carried 'en bandoulière' from the right shoulder to the left hip, and on the march strapped around the outer sides of the pack in an inverted 'U' manner. The Fähnrich or Ensign was extended the privilege of wearing the officers' Paletot, but with the pointed shoulder straps of the men.

Mecklenburg
As Prussia. Light green collar patches with white double Kapellen lace of reduced form and light green inner lights. Shoulder straps as on the tunic. NCO distinctions: White linen band with blue/yellow/carmine centrestripe. Buttons white.

Saxony
As Prussia. Black collar patches. NCO distinctions: White linen band with narrow green centrestripe. Shoulder straps as on tunic. Buttons white for Jäger, yellow for Schützen Regiment 108.

Bavaria
As Prussia. Light green collar patches. NCO distinctions: White linen band with narrow light blue centre stripe. Shoulder straps as on tunic. Buttons yellow.

Undress Tunic (Litewka)

Prussia
Derived from the word 'Litauen' and implying a loose fitting shapeless smock, the single-breasted Litewka was entirely of grey melton corresponding in colour to the greatcoat. Worn very much in the sense of a 'second-best' tunic, the coat was fastened by a concealed row of seven grey buttons, with plain sleeves without cuffs each provided at the rear with an adjustable grey cloth tab and button. The divided rear skirt without pocket flaps revealed two domed tombac buttons upon the waist seam with additional brass suspender hooks provided at each hip. A horizontal pocket flap without button was placed on each front skirt, and inner skirt pockets were also provided, the front left-hand containing the field dressings.

Dark green rectangular patches were displayed one each side of the stand-and-fall collar by the Guard and Line Jäger, black for the Guard Schützen outlined in red piping. The Guard adopted abbreviated double yellow lace upon the patch with red or black inner lights respectively. The Guard NCO adopted a single abbreviated lace.

Golden Oberjäger braid, 1.6cm wide, was applied to the front and base edge of the collar, patterned for the Guard, plain for the Line, square-cut in all cases. The Gefreiter displayed the small eagle button, the senior NCOs the large, positioned to the rear of the collar directly above and vertically in line with the shoulder button. The Feldwebel adopted on the left upper arm a triple chevron of golden braid, patterned or plain. Shoulder straps were red as on the tunic, for the Line with a yellow number or monogram, and for the Guard plain. All the customary insignia were displayed upon the Litewka shoulder straps, such as that of the One-year Volunteer, Re-enlisted Man, etc, and swallows' nests were basically grey with golden metallic trim. A black serge neck cloth was also worn beneath the collar.

Mecklenburg
As Prussia. Light green collar patches with abbreviated white double lace with light green inner lights. NCO collar buttons: Silver. Braid: Silver and patterned. Shoulder straps as on tunic.

Saxony
As Prussia. Dark green collar patches piped red. JB12, 13, NCO collar buttons and braid: Silver. Schützen Regiment 108, collar buttons and braid: Golden. Shoulder straps as on tunic.

Bavaria
Litewka as Prussia, but resembled the earlier 1900 pattern with additional breast pocket flaps and of light blue colour. Light green collar patches, NCO collar buttons and braid: Golden. Shoulder straps as on tunic.

Fatigue Dress (Drillichanzug)

Prussia
Officially described as light grey, but to all appearances white, the short single-breasted drill jacket was without a waist seam and fastened at the front by six zinc buttons. The sleeves were plain without cuffs, and shoulder straps were not displayed. Beneath the rounded 4cm high stand-up pattern collar a black neck cloth was well revealed. The jacket was without insignia except that the One-year Volunteer wore upon each shoulder a black and white twisted woollen cord extending from the shoulder button to the upper armhole seam. The Gefreiter also adopted around the base of the collar a narrow black twisted woollen cord.

A smarter single-breasted drill tunic was worn by the NCOs, fashioned on the lines of the tunic with fitted waist seam and divided rear skirt, but without tail pocket flaps and displaying only two belt supporter buttons on the rear waist seam. The drill tunic fastened by six domed yellow metal buttons, with the somewhat rounded front collar secured by two pairs of hooks and eyes. NCOs were further distinguished by a 0.7cm wide white linen border with 0.2cm wide black centre stripe placed around the front and upper edge of the collar and spaced 0.2cm from the outer edge. The established Feldwebel further displayed a 0.7cm wide white linen cuff ring with black centre stripe around each lower sleeve about 10cm from the base of the cuff. The trousers were of plain grey drill without piping and generally worn with black laced ankle boots but also, when occasion demanded, inside the marching boot. The soft visorless service cap was worn by the men with fatigue dress, but NCOs were permitted the peaked service cap.

Mecklenburg
As Prussia. NCO distinctions: White linen band with blue/yellow/carmine centre stripe. Gefreiter: Carmine twisted woollen cord around base of collar.

Saxony
As Prussia. NCO distinctions: White linen band with green centre stripe. Gefreiter: Green twisted woollen cord around base of collar.

Bavaria
As Prussia. NCO distinctions: White linen band with light blue centre stripe. Gefreiter: Light blue twisted woollen cord around base of collar.

6. MARKSMANSHIP AWARDS (Schützen Abzeichen)

General Marksmanship Cord (Allgemeine Schützenschnur)

Prussia
Introduced in 1894 the marksmanship cord represented the first time insignia in the imperial colours had been displayed upon the uniform. The award took the form of a black/white/red plaited woollen cord suspended from beneath the right-hand shoulder strap to the second front tunic, Litewka, or greatcoat button. At the upper or shoulder end of the cord was displayed a large oval woollen rosette, similarly interwoven in black/white/red, with attached to the lower end the initial grades of the award in the form of from 1 to 3 black/white/red woollen acorns. For the 4th grade a silver cord and rosette interwoven with black and red silk was substituted, but without any acorn award. The 5th grade additionally adopted a decorative brass shield or plaque mounted upon the rosette, which displayed the imperial crowned monogram WII enclosed within an oak leaf wreath, but still without any acorn award. For the 6th and 8th grades silver acorns appeared, interlaced with red and black silk. For the 9th and 10th grades, instituted in 1912, golden acorns were introduced. The individual grades of the award were as follows:

1. Black/white/red woollen cord, slides and rosette, with one woollen acorn.
2. As 1, with two woollen acorns.
3. As 1, with three woollen acorns.
4. Black/silver/red cord, slides and rosette, without acorn.
5. As 4, with addition of brass medallion.
6. As 5, with one silver acorn.
7. As 5, with two silver acorns.
8. As 5, with three silver acorns.
9. As 8, with the substitution of golden slides and one golden acorn.
10. As 9, with two golden acorns.

Mecklenburg
As Prussia.

Saxony
As Prussia but from 5th grade yellow metal plaque bearing royal crowned monogram FA within oak leaf wreath.

Bavaria
As Prussia but woollen cord, rosette, and acorns interwoven light blue/white for first three grades, with a silver cord interlaced with light blue silk for higher

grades. From 5th grade silver oval plaque bearing light blue/silver, diamond-patterned field. For 10th grade, golden oval plaque substituted around diamond field.

Emperor or King's Award (Kaiser/Königs Abzeichen)

Instituted in 1895 and awarded to the company within an army corps which, during a series of elimination contests, emerged with the highest standard of marksmanship, this was retained by the men for a year, but by the NCOs for the duration of their service with the company. Should the same company win the award three times then it became permanent insignia both for NCOs and men.

Prussia
Worn on the right upper tunic arm upon a dark green oval stiffened underlay, the badge entirely of brass displayed the skull of a royal stag bearing the antlers of a 'twelve-pointer' surmounted by a convex imperial crown. Upon the skull rested the cross of St Hubert with the date of the first award, placed on the brow of the skull, accentuated in a darker brass. Further dates were displayed to the left and the right of the skull. Due to the outbreak of war the badge was awarded for the last time in 1913 to the Third Company of Jäger Battalion 3.

Mecklenburg
As Prussia.

Saxony
As Prussia with substitution of king's crown.

Bavaria
As Prussia with substitution of king's crown and on a light blue oval cloth underlay.

7. COLOUR-BEARERS AND JÄGER FLAGS (Fahnenträger und Jägerfahnen

Sleeve Badge (Ärmel Abzeichen)

Prussia
Worn upon the right upper tunic sleeve, the badge depicted two crossed light yellow infantry flags embroidered on a dark green cloth underlay in the form of an heraldic shield. The flags, with upper tips slightly furled, each displayed a white field enclosed by a golden crowned laurel leaf wreath bearing the black Old Prussian flying eagle. A large yellow Prussian crown was placed between the upper intersection of the flag staffs with, between the lower, the large yellow initial W and small Roman numeral II. To the base of each spear point was attached an outwardly flowing tasselled riband in the appropriate black and white colours of Prussia. All detail upon the flags, the crowns, scrolls, grenades, corner monograms, wreaths and, in addition, the spear points and flag studs, was faithfully indicated and, to suggest gold, accentuated in a darker yellow ochre. The pearls around the crown arches and precious stones upon the crownband were simulated in white embroidery, the inner crown lining and

cushion displayed in red. In the event of the Emperor's Badge being awarded, normally displayed in the same position, this was mounted beneath the Colour-bearer's insignia.

Mecklenburg
Badge entirely of silver metal displaying crowned monogram FF enclosed within an oak leaf wreath and mounted on an oval dark green underlay.

Saxony
The Saxon Jäger, and Schützen Regiment 108, did not display flags.

Bavaria
The Bavarian Jäger did not display flags.

Gorget Plate (Ringkragen)

Prussia
The Colour-bearers were further distinguished by a crescent-shaped metal shield or gorget plate suspended upon the breast by an adjustable linked neck chain. A domed circular boss positioned in each upper rounded corner served to anchor the neck chain to the rear of the plate. The gorget rested between the first and third front tunic buttons with the top button remaining visible above the arched chamfer. At the rear the plate was stabilised by an elongated brass hook passed through the second buttonhole.

The tombac shield basically displayed the same devices as the sleeve badge, namely crossed flags with the Prussian crown above and royal monogram below. In effect there were certain differences, for example, the flags were crossed at a much lower angle while the ribands, in the case of the Line, flowed towards the centre and, for the Guard, hung vertically from the spear points, with all emblems upon the plates depicted in bold relief.

The neck chain was composed alternately of round and oval flat metal discs, each decorated respectively with a four- or six-sided arabesque design. The discs were each pierced top and bottom and interlinked with small metal rings, the entire chain corresponding in colour to the plate. Upon the greatcoat the gorget was adjusted to a higher position with the chain passing beneath the deep folded collar. The gorget plates of the Guard and Line were as follows:

(a) The Guard: Two crossed flags with, superimposed upon the intersection of the flag staffs, the eight-pointed Guard star surmounted by a small Prussian crown. Each domed anchor boss transformed into a bursting grenade by the addition, to the left, of an inverted cluster of laurel leaves and, to the right, of oak leaves. Plate of yellow metal for both the Guard Jäger and Guard Schützen.

(b) The Line: Two crossed flags with, superimposed upon the intersection of the flag staffs, the royal monogram WR without numeral, surmounted by a large Prussian crown. Each domed anchor boss transformed into a bursting grenade by the addition of an inverted cluster of combined oak and laurel leaves, the base flames of laurel, the rising flames of oak leaves. Plate of yellow metal for all Jäger battalions.

Mecklenburg
Two crossed Mecklenburg flags with, superimposed upon the intersection of the flag staffs, a crowned eight-pointed star bearing the circular inscription 'PER ASPERA AD ASTRA'. Plate of silver metal.

Bandolier (Fahnenbandolier)

Prussia

Emulating a pattern once carried by the flag officers of Frederick the Great, the bandolier was worn from the left shoulder to the right hip, passing beneath the gorget plate and over the leather waist belt. Basically of dark brown Morocco leather, the 11cm wide bandolier was faced with poppy red cloth for the Guard and Line Jäger, black velvet for the Guard Schützen, and bordered with a 4cm wide diagonally patterned golden braid. The facing cloth was revealed as a 2.5cm wide centre stripe between the braids and as a narrow trim beyond the braids. From the rounded base-join of the bandolier was suspended a roughly pear-shaped extension piece, similarly of dark brown Morocco leather, to which was attached a red Russia leather bucket shoe to support the flag staff.

Protective black waxed covers were also carried by the Colour-bearers, when not around the flag, from beneath the right shoulder to the left hip, crossing under the bandolier and leather waist belt. The tombac conical cap attached to the top of the flag cover and designed to enclose the decorative spear point rested in an inverted position on the left front tunic skirt. The cone was trimmed around the base with a decorative silver braid laced top and bottom with a 0.2cm black silk stripe and embossed on the front with a replica of the silver/black 1870 Iron Cross.

The bandolier itself was further provided with a black protective buttoned cover which, when not in use, was carried from the left shoulder to right hip beneath the bandolier.

Colour-bearers were also permitted a special elongated side-arm, straight-bladed and 78.7cm long, bearing the gilt basket hilt of the officers' '89 sword and carried in a black leather sheath with brass fittings. The Oberjäger side-arm tassel was tied to the hilt and not the frog but, in the event the Colour-bearer held the rank of Vizefeldwebel or above, the officers' sword and swordknot were carried.

Mecklenburg

Bandolier as Prussia except faced with light green velvet, bordered with silver patterned braid. Side-arm as Prussia except Mecklenburg coat of arms displayed in gilt basket hilt.

The Jäger Flags (Die Jägerfahnen)

Prussia

In 1914 the Jäger carried the 1890 flag pattern, each of equal dimension and 126cm square. Flagstaffs were yellow for the Guard and black for the Line, with a total length, including the spearhead, of about 300cm. The ornamental spear-point was entirely of gilt metal, bearing, in the centre, the black and silver Iron Cross of 1870/71, framed within a golden laurel leaf wreath. All flags adopted the so-called 'battalion ring' a highly polished brass cylindrical collar attached to the staff about 3.5cm beneath the flag cloth, inscribed with the initials of the battalion bearing the Colour. Line and Guard flags were as follows:

(a) The Line: The Line displayed a basically dark green flag carrying a circular white field from which emanated, to each corner, an expanding white chaplet, each outlined by a narrower black border defining the flag cloth as an equally proportioned Maltese Cross.

The field, enclosed within a golden crowned laurel leaf wreath bearing reddish-brown berries, displayed the black Old Prussian flying eagle with stylised red tongue, and crown, beak and talons of gold. In its right talon the eagle grasped an upright sword with silver blade and golden hilt, in its left a sheaf of golden forked lightning bolts. Placed above the eagle was a dark green scroll, outlined with a narrow golden/green twisted cord and inscribed with the golden motto 'PRO GLORIA ET PATRIA'.

In each corner of the flag, upon a dark green background was the crowned monogram WR encircled by a laurel leaf wreath in gold, while centrally between the monograms was depicted a golden flaming grenade. The orbs upon the crowns were light blue with golden cross and circlet, the pearls and precious stones around the crowns in silver, with inner linings of red. The eagle, though described as and appearing black, was in fact embroidered in its near-natural colours, that is shades of extremely dark brown.

(b) The Guard: The Guard Jäger carried by tradition a white flag additionally interwoven with long vertical golden threads with a dark green field enclosed within a golden crowned laurel leaf wreath bearing additional Rococco-style elaboration. The field displayed the customary crowned black Old Prussian flying eagle with upright sword and lightning bolts, except, to contrast against its dark background, the eagle's plumage was accentuated in golden embroidery. Above the eagle was the universal dark green scroll, outlined in gold, carrying the golden inscription 'PRO GLORIA ET PATRIA'. The corner monograms, also upon a dark green background, each displayed the golden monogram WR enclosed within a crowned golden wreath composed on one side of laurel and on the other of palm. In other respects, the flag conformed to the Line, except all ornament was heavily embroidered and of a more ornate form.

The Guard Schützen battalion displayed a similar flag, basically white with dark green field, but without the vertical golden threads and with the background of the corner monograms depicted in black, in other respects complying to the Guard Jäger.

Flag Ribbons (Fahnenbänder)

A decorative practice was the display of commemorative streamers or ribands tied in cravat fashion and suspended from the base of the spear point. These, in many cases, corresponded exactly to the actual ribbon of an order or decoration and fell into the following classifications:

1. Banner-ribbon (Banderole)

A 3.7cm wide ribbon vertically striped in the appropriate state colours, in the case of Prussia, black/silver/black/silver/black with additional narrow silver edging and terminating at each end in a black/silver tassel. Commemorative gilt clasps were attached to the ends of the ribbon, inscribed on the obverse with the crowned imperial monogram WRII and on the reverse with the foundation date of the battalion and the date '1. Januar 1900'.

2. Campaign Ribbons (Kriegsbänder)

(a) Ribbon of the Commemorative Campaign Medal (Kriegsgedenkmünze) 1813/14 or 1813/15: Orange ribbon with narrow white/black edging stripes. Carried by the Guard Jäger and JB1, 2, 5 and 6.

(b) Ribbon of the Military Decoration of Honour (Militärehrenzeichen) 1848/49: Black with narrow white/black edging stripes awarded with and without golden crossed swords. With swords carried by Guard Schützen Battalion and

JB5, without swords JB3, 7 and 8.

(c) Ribbon of the Commemorative Campaign Medal (Kriegsgedenkmünze) 1864: Black with a narrow white and a narrow orange stripe. Awarded with or without golden crossed swords. With swords carried by JB3 and 7.

(d) Ribbon of the Cross of Alsace (Alsenkreuzes) 1864: Dark blue with narrow black/white/orange edging stripes. Carried by JB3.

(e) Ribbon of the Commemorative Cross (Erinnerungskreuzes) 1866: Black with narrow orange/white edging stripes. Awarded with and without golden crossed swords. Carried by the Guard Jäger, Guard Schützen and JB1–8.

The ribbon of the War Commemorative Medal of 1870/71 was not adopted as the Jäger flags had not been carried under fire during the campaign.

3. Centennial Ribbons (Säkular Auszeichnungsbänder)
Awarded to the formations which had existed for a century, this was an approximately 10cm wide black ribbon with silver edging and silver fringes. Upon the ribbons embroidered in silver was displayed the foundation year of the battalion together with the initials of the founder and also the bestower of the ribbon. Carried by the Guard Jäger and JB1 displaying 'ERRICHTET 1744' and from 1908 by JB5 and 6 with '1808' and finally in 1914 by the Guard Schützen with '1814'. JB3, 4, 7 and 8 became eligible in 1915, but, due to the war, did not adopt the ribbon.

4. Ceremonial Ribbons (Paradebänder)
Of a special and individual pattern, presented by royal Colonels-in-Chief. JB6 awarded by Duke Ernst of Saxe-Altenburg the ribbon of the Order of the House of Ernestine with crossed silver swords. JB7 presented by Prince Adolf of Schaumburg-Lippe with the ribbon of the Military Distinguished Service Medal (Militärverdienst Medaille) and Queen Marguerita of Italy bestowed a ribbon upon JB11.

Mecklenburg

In keeping with its Guard status JB14 displayed a basically white flag bearing in the centre the grand ducal coat of arms surmounted by an ornamented helm and draped with the Collar of the Order of the Wendish Crown. In each corner of the flag was placed the golden crowned monogram FF enclosed within an intermixed golden/green wreath. The flag staff was white with gilt spear-point revealing the black/silver Iron Cross of 1870/71.

Flag Ribbons (Fahnenbänder)

1. Banner-ribbon (Banderole)
3.7cm wide and in the appropriate state colours red/yellow/blue/yellow/red ending in golden tassels. Commemorative gilt metal clasps inscribed on the obverse with crowned Grand Ducal monogram and on the reverse the foundation date of the battalion and the date '1 Januar 1900'.

2. Campaign Ribbons (Kriegsbänder)

(a) Ribbon of Prussian Commemorative Cross 1866 with golden swords: Black with narrow orange/white edging stripes.

(b) Mecklenburg Campaign Decoration (Kriegsauszeichnung) 1870/71: Ribbon blue/yellow/red/yellow/blue, with golden cross.

3. Ceremonial Ribbons (Paradebänder)
Two ribbons were presented to the battalion, one by the Mother Grand Duchess Alexandrine, the other by Grand Duchess Marie in 1881.

8. MUSICIANS & MUSIC MASTERS (Musiker und Musikmeister)

The Jäger music, of a totally different character to that of the infantry, was produced entirely by horn instruments, and there were no bandsmen or 'Spielleute' in the sense of drummers and fifers. Instead, each company had only buglers, employed in the field as signallers and traditionally entitled 'Flügelhornisten'. As a rule, the signal-buglers of the Line did not display swallows' nests and were mainly distinguishable by the short infantry-pattern bugle, wrapped with dark green cloth. An exception was formed by the buglers of the Guard who, when on ceremonial duties displayed red or black swallows' nests respectively, in both cases decorated with eight vertical yellow woollen bands horizontally trimmed by a single yellow band and with the addition of 3cm long yellow woollen fringes.

On the march the bugle was carried as by the infantry, by means of an adjustable red Russia leather strap passed under the left shoulder strap and clipped by snap hooks to the brass rings at each end of the bugle. The instrument was further supported by a shaped leather pad attached to the left side of the belt and additionally secured by a buckled leather strap. In the field, the bugle was carried slung around the neck. In practice all 'gelernt' Jäger, that is those who had followed a forestry vocation before enlistment, were equally trained in the Jäger hunting calls.

Twelve straight dark brown Antelope-horns presented by Emperor Wilhelm II in 1896, were carried by the buglers of the Guard Jäger on parade or festive occasions. They were carried over the left shoulder by a twisted dark green woollen cord, the same cord also binding the horn with the exception of the brass mouthpiece and upper sound-piece and ending in a single dark green acorn. The horn, about 100cm long, was retained in a vertical position, mouthpiece uppermost, by a black leather brass-buttoned strap attached to the badger flap.

Musicians (Musiker)

Prussia

The musicians were of NCO rank and entitled 'Waldhornisten' after the traditional forest or french horn. Their swallows' nests were basically red, or black for the Guard Schützen, trimmed with eight golden vertical braids horizontally edged with a single golden braid. The braid was plain for the Line, and the nests without fringes, but, for the Guard, patterned with 3cm long golden metallic fringes. When no fringe was displayed, a narrow, 0.2cm strip of poppy red remained visible beneath the horizontal braid.

A Jäger band averaged between 18–20 musicians, and woodwind instruments in the form of clarinet, flute, oboe and piccolo, or percussion, such as drums and cymbals, were not used. The principal instruments were the french horn, tuba, trombone, cornet, trumpet baritone (sousaphone) and Flügelhorn. A rare exception was formed by JB3 for some years unofficially carrying a base drum captured from the French in 1870/71 until finally approved as a battle honour by Emperor Wilhelm I. From 1908 all Bugle-Majors were re-entitled Music Master.

Mecklenburg
As Prussia. Light green swallows' nests. Waldhornist: Silver patterned Oberjäger braid with 3cm long silver fringes.

Saxony
As Prussia. Swallows' nests black. Buglers: White or yellow bands according to button colour. Waldhornist with gold or silver Oberjäger braid according to button colour. Schützen Regiment 108 possessed 48 buglers, four to each company carrying the infantry pattern bugle. On parade these marched in mass assembly under the leadership of the Music Master at the head of the regiment. The Music Master carried a silver bugle wrapped with dark green cords and tassels interwoven with gold.

Bavaria
As Prussia. Light green swallows' nests. Buglers: Yellow bands. Waldhornist: Golden Oberjäger braid. Bugle cords light green.

There is evidence to suggest that even after 1908, when the title Music Master was officially adopted, that the older pattern swallows' nests continued to be worn for some time. For this reason details of the old Bugle-Major swallows' nests are given below:

Prussia
Battalion Bugle-Majors of both Guard and Line were distinguished by 7cm long metallic fringes.

Mecklenburg
7cm long silver fringes.

Saxony
7cm long silver or gold fringes.

Bavaria
7cm long gold fringes.

Music Masters (Musik Meister)

Prussia
The dress of the Music Master was almost identical to that of the officer, but retained a number of peculiarities. The tunic adopted the better cut and finer material, but the collar, while higher than the NCOs', was significantly not quite so high as the officer's. The Music Masters of the Guard did not display the officers' golden collar and cuff embroidery, but instead the lace pattern of the men, with red or black inner lights, though of somewhat larger form and woven of golden silk. The so-called Music Masters' girdle, was also adopted, based on the officers' Feldbinde, but wider, and entirely of poppy red cloth bordered top and bottom with silver Music Master braid, each laced with two 0.2cm wide black silk stripes. This in reality corresponded to the epaulette braid of the officer. The narrow vertical slides each side of the buckle were similarly faced with the same silver braid. The gilt circular buckle also resembled the officers', but displayed the traditional Greek lyre superimposed upon crossed swords enclosed within a raised laurel leaf wreath.

The woollen triple plaited shoulder cord on a stiffened underlay superficially suggested the staff officers' but was of a completely different weave entirely of poppy red, and conformed in size to the company officers'. A gilt battalion number, or crowned monogram for JB11, of the small 1.8cm size, was displayed upon the centre of the cords with, beneath, a gilt metal lyre, without swords. After five years' service, the Music Master was eligible for promotion to Obermusikmeister or Senior Music Master and in this event the centre cord of the triple weave was replaced by one of metallic gold.

Swallows' nests were also of a universal Music Master pattern, basically of poppy red cloth for the Guard and Line Jäger, black for the Guard Schützen, trimmed with eight vertical bands, each terminating at the base in the pointed Old Prussian manner. Each vertical band displayed the silver Music Master braid and was horizontally bordered by a narrow 0.4cm twisted silver cord from which were suspended 7cm long thin metallic fringes, universally of silver regardless of button colour.

The officers' light grey paletot was adopted, conforming in all respects except that the dark green collar, when in the raised position, revealed the grey material of the coat and not the poppy red lining of the officer. Swallows' nests were not adopted upon the paletot. Similarly the dark green Überrock fully conformed to the officers' pattern though always with a cloth, not velvet, collar and differed in the display of poppy red shoulder cords. The Überrock served admirably as a frock coat when conducting at concerts, etc. Also adopted was the officers' high stiff-shafted black leather boot but without spurs. The body sash and cape were not adopted, but gloves corresponded, of white leather for parade and reddish-brown for service occasions and the officers' shako was worn with red buffalo hair plumes.

The universal pattern '89 sword was carried, suspended in the underslung manner of the officer from a leather or webbing belt beneath the tunic, with sling of plain black patent leather, without the officers' gold or silver braid.

Mecklenburg
Swallows' nests: Light green. Music Master braid: Silver laced with two carmine silk stripes. Waist girdle: Light green with Music Master braid. Red shako plume.

Saxony
Swallows' nests: Black. Music Master braid: Silver laced with two green silk stripes. Waist girdle: Black with Music Master braid. Black shako plume.

Bavaria
Swallows' nests: Light green. Music Master braid: Silver laced with two light blue silk stripes. Waist girdle: Light green with Music Master braid. No shako plume.

9. SIDE-ARM KNOTS (Hirschfänger-Troddeln)

Prussia
For the Jägerman, all parts of the side-arm knot, that is the linen strap with attached woollen slide, stem, crown and loose-fringed tassel, were entirely dark green. The Oberjäger displayed a dark green strap edged each side with two silk silver stripes, the slide, stem and crown remaining basically of dark green, but interwoven with silver silk, with the loose tassel composed of intermixed green

and silver fringes. Re-enlisted men displayed a dark green strap and slide, but with the stem and crown interwoven in the white/black colours of Prussia with white loose woollen tassel inner filled black. In all cases the strap was tied to the black leather bayonet frog, free of the side-arm and suspended to the front of the bayonet with its upper slide 6cm beneath the crossguard. The Fähnrich, Vize-feldwebel and Feldwebel carried the officers' swordknot tied to the sword hilt.

Mecklenburg

(a) Men: Dark green as Prussia.

(b) Oberjäger: Dark green strap edged each side with two golden silk stripes. The slide, stem and crown basically of dark green interwoven with golden silk. Acorn gilt, inner filled green/gold.

(c) Re-enlisted Man: Dark green strap and slide, stem and crown interwoven blue/yellow/carmine. Mixed blue/yellow/carmine tassel.

Saxony

(a) Men: Dark green as Prussia.

(b) Oberjäger: As Prussia.

(c) Re-enlisted Man: Dark green strap and slide. Stem and crown interwoven white/green. White tassel, inner filled green.

Schützen Regiment 108

(a) Men: As infantry. Stem in battalion colour (white, red or yellow), slide and crown in company colours (white, red, yellow or light blue). The slide and crown in combination with the stem effected a different colour sequence each time. Linen strap and woollen tassel universally white.

(b) Unteroffizier: White linen strap edged each side with two green silk stripes. Woollen slide, stem and crown interwoven in white/green. Loose white woollen tassel inner filled green.

(c) Re-enlisted Man: White strap. Slide in battalion colour with undulating centre stripe in company colour. Stem and crown interwoven white/green. Tassel white, inner filled green.

Bavaria

(a) Men: As infantry. Stem in battalion colour, slide and crown in company colours. Strap and loose tassel white.

(b) Oberjäger: White linen strap edged each side with two light blue stripes. Slide and stem interwoven white/light blue. Crown light blue with undulating white centre stripe. Tassel white, inner filled light blue.

(c) Re-enlisted Man: White strap. Slide in battalion colour with undulating centre stripe in company colour. Stem interwoven white/light blue, crown light blue with undulating white centre stripe. Tassel white, inner filled light blue.

10. EQUIPMENT (Ausrüstung)

Service Belt (Koppel)

Prussia

Of universal pattern throughout the army the black leather waist belt was secured by a highly polished brass rectangular buckle embossed in the centre with a domed circular shield of German silver. The centre of the shield displayed the royal Prussian crown enclosed within a raised circular scroll defined by two spirally twisted rings, bearing in the upper half the block-lettered inscription 'GOTT MIT UNS', and in the lower half two individual laurel leaf palms with stems entwined at the base. Worn correctly the belt buckle fully obscured the lowest front tunic button and the belt, at the rear, rested upon the two button-hooks provided. For walking out purposes a so-called 'garrison' belt of black patent leather could be privately purchased, but it was not permitted for normal service wear. The belt was worn by all ranks up to Feldwebel.

Senior NCOs carried the officers' sword externally suspended from the left side of the belt by a single black leather sling with, to the front of this a brass suspender hook, the so-called 'ducks-beak', supported on a short brass chain enabling the sword to be clipped in a vertical position.

Mecklenburg
As Prussia. Brass rectangular buckle displaying white metal eight-pointed star bearing the grand ducal state coat of arms. No inscription carried.

Saxony
As Prussia. By Jäger battalions, white metal rectangular buckle embossed with a domed circular brass shield displaying the royal Saxon crown and block-lettered inscription 'PROVIDENTIAE MEMOR'. By the Schützen Regiment 108 brass rectangular buckle with white metal domed plate bearing crowned monogram G, enclosed by only a single spirally twisted ring and with somewhat abbreviated laurel leaf pelms.

Bavaria
As Prussia. Brass rectangular buckle with circular domed plate of German silver displaying the royal Bavarian crown and block-lettered inscription 'IN TREUE FEST', with laurel leaf palms below.

Side-arm (Hirschfänger)

The infantry pattern '98 sword bayonet was carried designated either the S98 nA (new pattern) or S98 aA (old pattern), in practice differing from each other only in the grip construction. The grip of the new pattern comprised two separate dark brown wooden plates inset into the steel handle and bolted together, whereas that of the old was made entirely of one piece. Both patterns of bayonet possessed the distinctive 'eagles beak' pommel with an abbreviated steel cross-guard upswept to the front, and a total length of 69cm of which the single-edged steel blade comprised 52.5cm. The black leather sheath, with fittings of natural steel, was supported in a black leather frog looped from the left side of the belt. The MG companies carried the older modified pattern 71/84 bayonet.

Ammunition Pouches (Patronentaschen 1895)

Universally of black leather and of a low rectangular pattern, two pouches were carried, looped to the belt one each side of the buckle and each containing 45 rounds. They differed from previous patterns in that the side straps were no longer stitched to the shallow hinged lid, but instead to the deep side walls of the pouch. In cases where pouches were not worn, black leather belt loops were substituted, each provided with a rectangular brass buckle enabling the pack straps to be attached.

Haversack (Brotbeutel Pattern 1893)

Universally of plain reddish-brown canvas, the haversack normally rested upon the right rear hip suspended from the waist belt by means of two buttoned loops and stabilised in the centre by a brass hook. The outer flap extended to the base of the haversack and when fastened only the tips of the inner-stitched brown leather straps remained visible. A permanently attached metal ring and brown leather loop provided on the left side of the flap served to attach the water bottle. All buttons, buckles, etc., were of brass. An adjustable brown leather shoulder strap was also provided to carry the haversack when the belt was not worn, a method generally only adopted within camp confines or on fatigue duties. An aluminium drinking cup with foldable wire frame handles was also carried in the haversack.

Water-Bottle (Feldflasche Pattern 1893)

Entirely of aluminium, oval in shape, with a convex front and flat back, the flask was contained within a greyish-brown felt cover fastened by four small buttons covered in the same material. Supported within a black leather strap and carried attached to the left-hand side of the haversack, the bottle was provided with a metal screw cap with cork inlay. Capacity: 1 litre.

Medical personnel carried in addition the so-called 'Labeflasche' or literally 'reviving flask'. An enlarged version of the normal water bottle carried by an adjustable leather strap from the left shoulder and clipped by a brass hook at the rear to the right-hand side of the belt. The bottle possessed a more convenient oval drinking beaker strapped in an inverted manner on top of the bottle.

Mess Tin (Kochgeschirr Pattern 1910)

Of blackened aluminium and oval in shape, the 'Kochgeschirr' was strapped horizontally on the upper pack flap with the lid to the right. Composed of two parts, a deep base forming a soup or stew container, with an attached wire frame handle, and a shallow press-fit lid which transformed into a small frying pan by means of an attached spring-loaded handle which, when collapsed, also served to clamp the utensils together. The combined spoon and fork was generally carried in the neck of the mess tin.

Entrenching Tool (Schanzzeug)

Short-handled spade supported blade uppermost in a black leather frame hold-all from the left-hand side of the belt by two black leather loops. The handle was of natural-coloured wood ending in a ball grip and cross-strapped to the bayonet sheath.

Bivouac Sheet (Zeltbahn)

Introduced in 1892, and of reddish-brown canvas the bivouac sheet was carried strapped around the outer edges of the pack on top of the greatcoat. Accessories such as tent pegs, guy ropes, poles etc, were carried separately in a special canvas wallet within the pack. From 1911 the reddish-brown tent sheet commenced to be replaced by one of field grey.

Pack (Tornister or Dachs Pattern 1895/97)

Prussia
Conformed to infantry pattern, but basically of black leather with the rear and side walls covered in black calfhide and the outer flap in black, or blackish-brown, badger-skin with, in addition, upon the flap, a black/silvery-grey badger head with imitation red leather eyes and for this reason entitled the 'Dachs' or 'badger'. The pack was supported by black leather adjustable straps based on the 'Y' system of suspension and the attached greatcoat and mess tin straps were similarly of black leather. Fähnrich and Senior NCOs were excused the pack. The Cyclist companies carried a rucksack of plain reddish-brown canvas material supported by black leather straps.

Mecklenburg
As Prussia.

Saxony
Of infantry pattern, covered in black calfhide, black leather support straps.

Bavaria
Of infantry pattern, covered in reddish-brown calfhide. Black leather support straps.

Rifle (Gewehr or 'Büchse' '98)

The standard infantry rifle of 7.92mm calibre and Mauser design with an internal not external magazine holding a clip of five rounds. The barrel, with its attached metal fittings, was of blued steel, the breech mechanism together with the straight, not inclined, bolt handle of natural steel, with wooden stock and hand-guard left in its light brown condition. Without side-arm the rifle was 125cm long, with side-arm 177cm, weighed 4.1kg and sights were graduated from 200–2,000 metres. The rifle sling of red Russia leather with use became dark brown in shade. The Cyclist battalions were equipped with the 110cm long carbine M/98 with a weight of 3.8kg.

Machine-Gun (Maxim pattern 1908)

Designated the MG 08 and of 7.92mm calibre, this was a water-cooled belt-fed weapon, each belt holding 250 rounds, with a rate of fire between 400–500 rounds per minute and maximum range of 4000 metres. A machine-gun company comprised six guns, each normally manned by a crew of five and with a total weight of 53kg capable of being drawn over reasonable terrain, by means of its sledge carriage, by only two men. The Jäger machine-gun companies wore the uniform of their parent battalion distinguished by the Arabic company number 5 upon the shoulder strap buttons, and in the field by a dark brown leather 'Trägegurt' or gunsling worn, bandolier fashion, from the left shoulder to the right hip. The machine-gunners were principally armed with the pistole 08 Parabellum (Mauser) for self protection, but to a certain extent rifles were also carried.

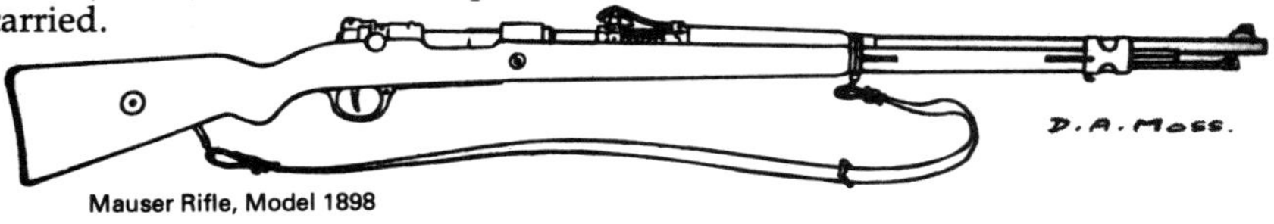

Mauser Rifle, Model 1898

11. HEAD-DRESS (Kopfbedeckung)

Service Caps (Mütze)

Prussia
For the men the caps were of a low visorless pattern, with the diameter of the crown only slightly exceeding that of the headband. The cap cloth corresponded to the colour of the tunic and the capband to the colour of the tunic collar while a thin strip, about 0.2cm, of the basic cap material remained visible beneath the narrow band. In the centre of the front crown cloth was displayed the imperial black/white/red cockade with, directly beneath, in the centre of the capband, the individual state cockade in its appropriate colours. The cockades of the men, each 2cm in diameter, were simply of enamelled metal with yellow generally simulated by brass. NCOs were permitted the so-called 'extra cap' of finer material and slightly stiffer construction with better quality cockades and the addition of a black leather peak. For walking out purposes this cap was also privately purchased by the men. The Fähnrich, Vizefeldwebel and Feldwebel always wore the peaked cap with the cockades of the officer. The caps were as follows:

(a) Guard Jäger and Line Battalions 1–11: Dark green crown cloth, poppy red capband with poppy red piping around the crown seam. Upper cockade: Black/white/red. Lower cockade: Black/white/black.

(b) Guard Schützen: Dark green crown cloth, black capband, piped red top and bottom and around the crown seam. Upper cockade: Black/white/red. Lower cockade: Black/white/black.

(c) Jäger Battalion 7; (Schaumburg-Lippe): As Line Jäger but lower cockade white/red/white.

Mecklenburg
Dark green crown cloth, light green capband, piped red top and bottom and around crown seam. Upper cockade: Black/white/red. Lower cockade: Blue/yellow/carmine.

Saxony
Dark green (extremely dark) crown coth, black capband, piped red top and bottom and around the crown seam. Upper cockade: Black/white/red. Lower cockade: White/green/white.

Bavaria
Light blue crown cloth, light green capband with light green piping around crown seam. Upper cockade: Black/white/red. Lower cockade: White/blue/white.

Shako (Tschako)

Prussia
Based on the 1860 pattern, but since 1888 reduced in height, the shako was entirely of highly polished black leather with rounded front and rear peaks, without metallic trim and, from 1895, without the leather baseband of the officer. A black lacquered metal ventilation grille was provided at each upper side of the shako. The chinstrap of plain black leather, with two adjustable brass sliding buckles, secured each side by plain brass chinstrap bosses with, beneath the right-hand boss, the imperial black/white/red cockade. Upon the front of the shako the Guard displayed in German silver the eight-pointed Guard star with,

around the outer points of the star, a silver circular scroll inscribed with the words 'MIT GOTT FUR KOENIG UND VATERLAND' [spelling as on scroll inscription] and at the base the date '1860'.

For the Line, the shako plates were of dark bronzed metal, the Battalions 1, 2, 5 and 6 displaying the old 'Grenadier' eagle bearing the monogram FWR upon an oval breast shield, and the Battalions 3, 4, 7, 8, 9, 10 and 11 the 'Line' eagle displaying the initials FR, accentuated in darker bronze, upon its breast. In both cases the heraldic eagle grasped an orb in its left talon, and a sceptre in its right, and displayed, since 1860, a stylised scroll flowing across the breast and wings bearing the inscription 'MIT GOTT FUR KOENIG UND VATERLAND', often entitled the 'Fatherland Scroll'. JB10 additionally displayed around the eagle a circular scroll, awarded in 1899, bearing in blackened lettering the battle honours 'Waterloo/Peninsula/Venta del Pozo'.

At the top of the shako, positioned in the centre and half projecting above the brim, was the oval fieldbadge, entirely of coloured cloth with inner field of black and outer border of white. JB7 displayed the colours of Schaumburg-Lippe in the triple combination white/red/blue. In all cases the rear of the fieldbadge was generally simply of black cloth.

On parade all battalions displayed black horsehair plumes, red for the musicians, or red buffalo-hair for the Music Master, supported on a plain brass plume holder secured behind the fieldbadge and somewhat curved to the front, the base of the plume hanging level with the upper seam of the front peak. The Signal-Buglers, as the men, displayed black plumes similarly retained by brass plume buttons, whereas those of the NCOs and musicians were enamelled white. In the field a grey-green linen cover officially described as 'Schilf' or rush green without battalion numbers was worn over the shako and clipped to the front and rear peaks with only the fieldbadge displayed. On manoeuvres the aggressive or 'red party' was distinguished by a wide red band around the base of the cover. Music Masters were permitted the gilt chinscales and silver/black fieldbadge of the officer.

Mecklenburg

As Prussia. Shako plate: Twelve-rayed tombac heraldic sun with abbreviated base bearing crowned state coat of arms within a laurel leaf wreath in German silver. All metal fittings of tombac. Plume retainer button: Enamelled white. Fieldbadge: Outer border white, inner field quartered carmine/dark blue, superimposed with yellow cross enclosed within a yellow woollen oval.

Saxony

Shako of low Keppi pattern with black leather straight-fronted peak but without rear peak. Chinstrap of black leather with metal buckles and chinstrap bosses in button colour. Beneath the right-hand boss, the imperial black/white/red cockade; beneath the left, the Saxon white/green/white; both cockades with smooth, not serrated outer rim. Fieldbadge not displayed. Shako covered in black cloth displaying, for JB12 and 13, an eight-pointed star of German silver bearing the crowned state coat of arms enclosed within a laurel leaf wreath with hunting horn upon the base in tombac. Colours reversed for Schützen Regiment 108 with tombac star and German silver coat of arms and hunting horn. For all battalions black shako plume bound in a bow at left-hand side and retained by a small black leather buckled strap. For JB12 a rising plume, JB13 a drooping plume and Schützen Regiment 108 a horizontal plume. Around the top of the shako the

Illustrations on facing and following pages:

Plate A

1. Swallows' Nest (Waldhornist—Guard Schützen, Prussia)
2. Shoulder Cord (Music Master—Guard Jäger or Guard Schützen, Prussia)
3. Swallows' Nest (Waldhornist—Mecklenburg)
4. Waist Girdle (Music Master—Prussia)
5. Swallows' Nest (Music Master—Prussia)

6, 7, 8. Music Master Braid (Bavaria, Saxony, Mecklenburg)

9. Centre Field of Belt Buckle (Music Master—Prussia)
10. Gorget (Colour-bearer—Guard Jäger, Prussia)
11. Waist Girdle (Music Master—Saxony)

12, 13, 14, 15. Fieldbadges (Prussia, Schaumberg, Mecklenburg, Bavaria)

16. Marksmanship Cord, 2nd Class (Prussia)
17. Sleeve Badge (Colour-bearer—Prussia)
18. Marksmanship Cord, 2nd Class (Bavaria)
19. Emperor's Badge (Prussia)
20. King's Badge (Bavaria)

Plate B—Flags
top: Guard Schützen (Prussia)
bottom: Line Jäger (Westphalia JB7)

Plate C—Colour-bearers
left: Manoeuvre Dress (Mecklenburg)
right: Field Marching Order (Prussia)

Plate D—Officers' Dress

Plate E
from left to right:
Parade Dress (Waldhornist—Prussia)
Walking Out Dress (One-year Volunteer—Prussia)
Walking Out Greatcoat (Jäger—Prussia)

Plate F
from left to right:
Manoeuvre Dress (Signal-bugler—Mecklenburg)
Field Marching Order (Jäger—Saxony)
Field Marching Order (Jäger—Prussia)

Plate G—Grey-green Field Dress 1914
from left to right:
Major (Guard Jäger—Prussia)
Gefreiter (MG Company JB10—Prussia)
Oberjäger (Medical Section JB11, Reserve—Prussia)

SADDLE CLOTHS

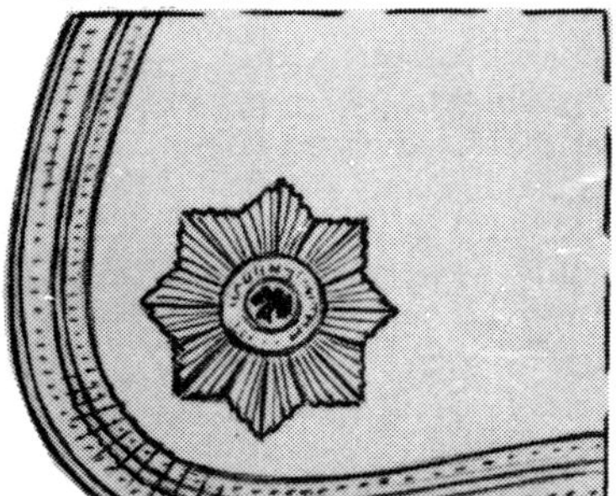

Parade Saddle Cloth (Guard)

Parade Saddle Cloth (Line)

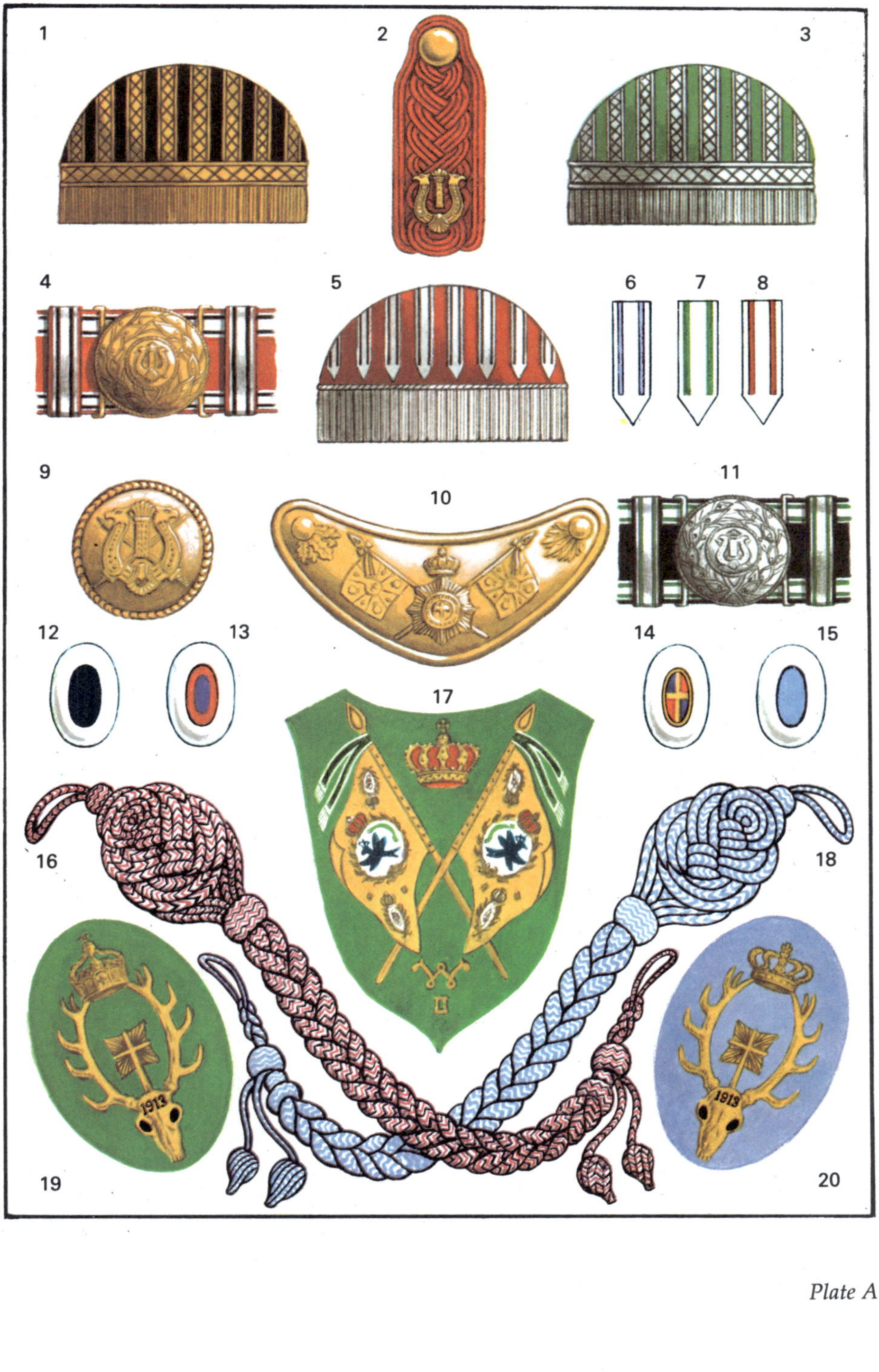

Plate A

ERRICHTET 1814.
GARDE-SCHÜTZEN-BATAILLON.
F.W.
W II
PRO GLORIA ET PATRIA
Auxerre.
Piemont.
Grave.
Marnoy.
La Grange.
Chatillon.
Vorges.
D.A. MOSS 1976.

Plate B

Plate C

Plate D

Parade Dress (Ma

Undress Topcoat (Hauptmann—Prussia)

Walking Out Dress (Hauptmann—Bavaria)

Parade Dress (Oberleutnant—Guard Schützen, Prussia)

utant—Prussia)

Service Dress, Paletot (Major—Prussia)

Service Dress (Oberleutnant—Saxony)

Undress (Hauptmann—Mecklenburg)

Undress Paletot (Ensign—Prussia)

Undress, Litewka (Hauptmann—Saxony)

Plate E

Plate F

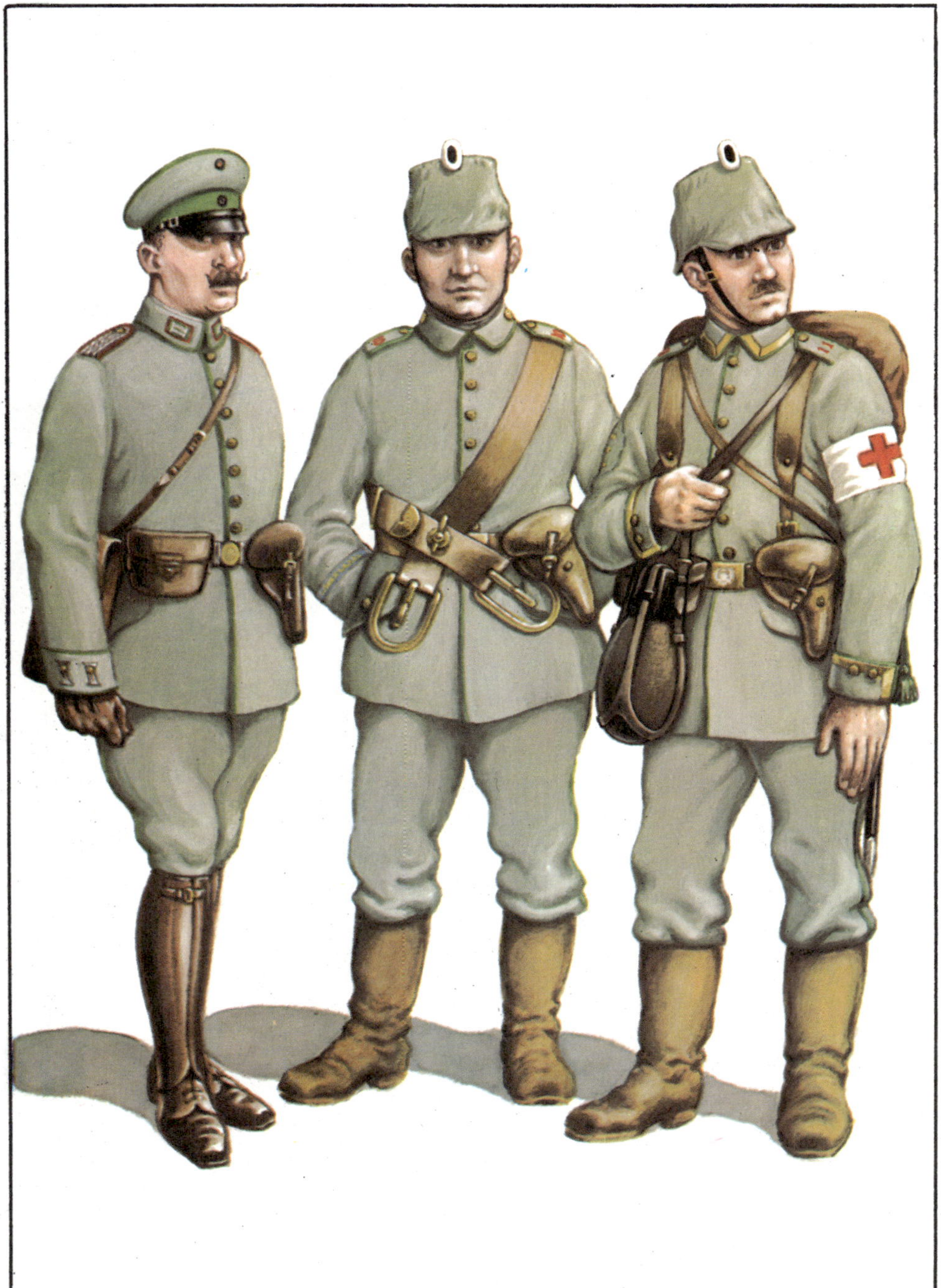

Plate G

Oberjäger displayed one silver braid ring, the Vizefeldwebel and Feldwebel two silver braid rings. Schützen Regiment 108 substituted golden braid rings. With exception of parade and orderly dress the basically felt shako always protected within a black waxed cloth cover with provision to display the plume. In the field, grey/green linen cover substituted without number. An exception was formed by Schützen Regiment 108 which, as the infantry, displayed their red number upon the cover.

Bavaria

As Prussia. Shako adopted in 1896. Shako plate: Tombac state coat of arms with crowned lion supporters mounted upon a scroll bearing the inscription 'IN TREUE FEST'. All metal fittings of tombac with, since February, 1914, black leather chinstraps. Beneath the right-hand chinstrap boss, the imperial black/white/red cockade. Fieldbadge: Outer border white, inner field light blue. Shako plume not displayed. In the field, grey/green linen cover worn.

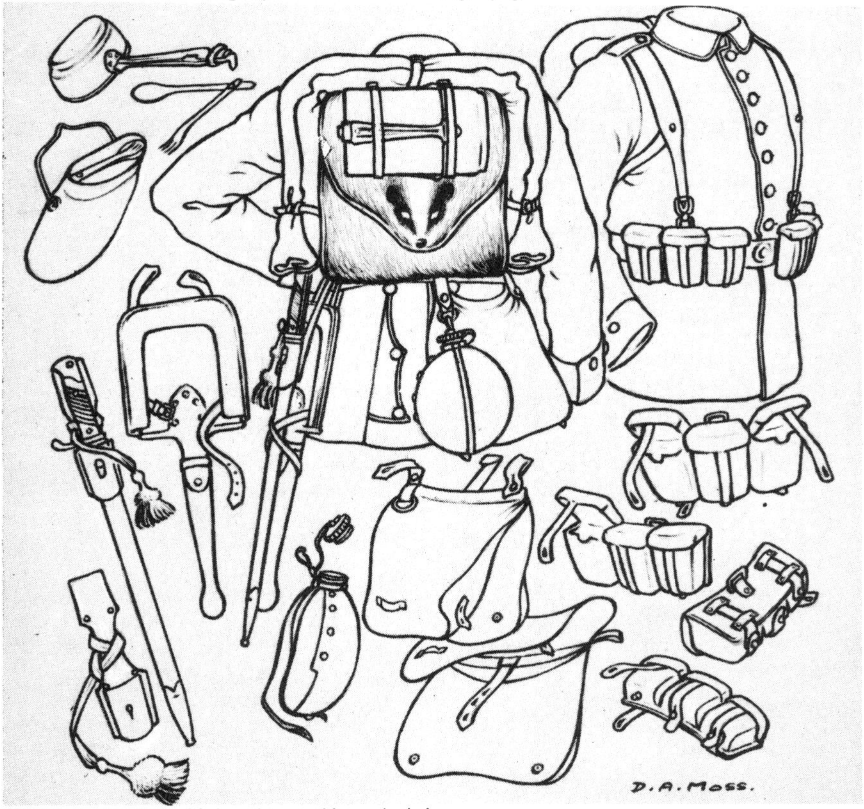

Top centre: Rear view of full service marching order being worn.
Top right: Front view of full service marching order.
Bottom right: Four views of pattern '09 ammunition pouches.
Bottom centre: Two views of haversack and side view of water-bottle.
Bottom left: Bayonet frog.
Centre left: Bayonet and entrenching spade.
Top left: Mess tins.

SECTION II

Officers

1. THE TUNIC (Waffenrock)

Prussia

Of universal pattern both for officers and men, in practice the officers' tunic, in addition to its superior cut and appreciably lighter shade of green, retained a number of individual features. The stand-up poppy red collar, secured by three pairs of hooks and eyes, and of black velvet for the Guard Schützen, was of a distinctly higher and stiffer pattern than the men's, though not exceeding a height of 6cm, and similarly square-fronted for the Guard and half-rounded for the Line. As for the men, the front and upper edge of the collar was additionally piped in dark green, poppy red for the Schützen, with a protective black silk neckband just visible above the upper collar line. The domed tunic buttons followed the sequence of the men's, that is eight down the front and six on the tail pocket flaps, but in all cases of gilt metal, the small 1.9cm diameter shoulder buttons remaining plain without company numbers.

Upon each shoulder was a permanently attached epaulette bridle each representing a loop of poppy red cloth faced with 1.6cm silver epaulette braid laced each side with a 0.2cm black silk stripe. When shoulder cords were worn the epaulette bridles remained visible beneath, extending about 0.5cm each side of the cords. A cloth loop in the dark green colour of the tunic was provided at each upper armhole seam through which the base tongue of the detachable shoulder cords was passed.

Sleeve cuffs corresponded to the men's, either of the Swedish pattern, with two horizontal buttons or, for the Guard Schützen, the French or arched Brandenburg with three vertical buttons. In both cases of larger dimension than the men's, with an 8cm cuff and a 14cm high and 7cm wide rectangular sleeve patch, including piping.

The officers of the Guard were distinguished by a golden Kapellen embroidery; upon the collar of elongated double form revealing respectively a red or black centre-dart with the upper and lower inner lights replaced by a golden double twisted cord. Each cuff embroidery was of more abbreviated form, displayed upon the Swedish as two single vertical laces, and upon the arched sleeve patch as three single horizontal laces with inner light in each case replaced by a golden twisted cord. In all cases the base of the chaplets was further defined by a golden twisted cord and the lace was of an appropriately larger dimension than the men's.

All tunic pipings were 0.2cm wide and of poppy red cloth extending the full length of the tunic front on the buttonhole side and outlining each of the arched tail pocket flaps. The uppermost waist buttons remained of normal button pattern and the divided rear skirt was lined with black silk. Unlike the men, the back section of the tunic was cut from two pieces with a vertical centre seam. The officers of JB10 similarly adopted the narrow light blue band around the lower right sleeve bearing in golden embroidery the block-lettered inscription 'GIBRALTAR', and the officers of JB11 a gilt crowned monogram M upon the shoulder cords.

Mecklenburg
As Prussia. Light green square-fronted collar, piped red around front, upper and base edge, and light green Swedish cuffs piped red around upper and rear edge. Silver buttons. Silver collar and cuff embroidery, inner lights of silver twisted cord, light green centre dart. Collar and cuff facings of a particularly light shade of grass green.

Saxony
As Prussia. Black velvet rounded-front collar piped red around all edges, black velvet German cuffs piped red. JB12, 13: Silver buttons. Schützen Regiment 108: Gilt buttons. Battalion numbers silver or gilt.

Bavaria
As Prussia, but traditionally, since 1815, of infantry light blue. Light green rounded-front collar piped light blue around front and upper edge. Light green Swedish cuffs. Light green piping down tunic front and around arched tail pocket flaps. Buttons and battalion numbers gilt.

2. RANK INSIGNIA (Dienstgradabzeichen)

Epaulettes (Epauletten)

Prussia
The epaulette, purely an article of parade or ceremonial wear, comprised a square-ended shoulder strap with diagonally cut upper corners, enlarging at the base into a large elliptical field enclosed within a smooth and highly polished gilt half-moon or crescent. The strap, bordered with silver epaulette braid, 1.6cm wide and laced each side with a 0.2cm black silk stripe, was retained at the base by the bridle and secured at the upper end by the domed shoulder button. The field of the epaulette corresponded in colour to the men's shoulder straps, that is poppy red, and the whole piece was mounted on a poppy red foundation cloth which extended beyond the outer edges of the epaulette as a narrow trim.

Battalion numbers and monograms were of gilt metal and displayed vertically in the centre of the field with the crown of the monogram positioned between the points of the crescent with its tip resting on the epaulette bridle. The numerals, of large 3.5cm size, displayed patterned upper surfaces enclosed within a smoothly polished outer border, whereas the monogram of JB11 was cast in the distinctive block-lettered form with the additional elaboration reserved for foreign Colonels-in-chief.

Rank stars were universally of gilt metal and positioned with one point towards the shoulder button, normally measuring 1.8cm across opposite points. The company officers, that is up to Captain, displayed epaulettes without fringes, but staff officers, that is from Major upwards, adopted thin silver metallic cords, or 'Cantillen', 7.5cm long. Reserve officers displayed gilt Arabic army corps numbers upon the epaulette. The individual rank grades upon the epaulette were indicated as follows:

(a) Leutnant (Second-Lieutenant): Without star. Battalion number or monogram only. No fringe.

(b) Oberleutnant (Lieutenant): One rank star placed below battalion number or monogram. No fringe.

(c) Hauptmann (Captain): Two rank stars placed one each side of battalion number or monogram. No fringe.

(d) Major (Major): Without star, battalion number or monogram only. In addition, thin silver fringes.

(e) Oberstleutnant (Lieutenant Colonel): One rank star placed below battalion number or monogram. In addition, thin silver fringes.

(f) Oberst (Colonel): Two rank stars placed one each side of battalion number or monogram. In addition, thin silver fringes.

Active Generals did not number among the Jäger, but royal Colonels-in-Chief were entitled 'Generals à la suite' or Generals belonging to the entourage serving in an honorary or advisory capacity. They retained the epaulettes of the staff officer but replaced the thin silver fringes with the stiff silver coils or 'bouillons' of the Infantry General. Lady Colonels-in-Chief, such as Queen Marguerita, did not display General rank, but instead that of a staff officer, usually Major. Battalion number or monogram was retained.

Shoulder Cords (Achselstücke)

Prussia

The shoulder cords of the company officer appeared as four silver braided cords laid tightly side by side, composed of an inner and outer cord each formed into a rounded loop at their upper end and returned on themselves. The buttonhole was formed in the centre cord with each cord formed of two narrower strands stitched together in the alternate manner termed Russia braid. The individual cords were 1cm wide and flecked at 1cm intervals with black silken threads giving an overall herringbone effect. The cords were directly stitched to a poppy red cloth underlay which extended beyond the cords in the manner of a narrow piping.

All rank stars and battalion numbers were of gilt metal, for the company officers of the small size, with the stars positioned with one point towards the shoulder button.

For the staff officers, a more elaborate shoulder cord was devised composed of two silver braided cords laid tightly side by side, interwoven in a basketweave manner to form five even curves at each side, two at the base and a single elongated loop at the upper end through which the shoulder button was passed. The cords were similarly flecked at 1cm intervals with black silk and placed on a stiffer and slightly wider poppy red underlay extending about 0.2cm each side of the cords and giving a total width of 5.5cm. For the staff officers gilt battalion numbers and rank stars were of medium size. The individual rank upon the shoulder-cords was indicated as follows:

(a) Leutnant and Major: Without rank stars. Regimental number or monogram only.

(b) Oberleutnant and Oberstleutnant: One rank star placed below numeral or monogram.

(c) Hauptmann and Oberst: Two rank stars, placed one above and one below the number or monogram.

Generals' à la suite shoulder cords conformed to the active Generals' comprising three metallic cords interwoven to form four even curves at each side, two at the base, and a single large upper loop which encompassed the shoulder button. The two outer cords, each 0.6cm wide, were of gold, the inner cord, of silver and 0.5cm wide, was additionally flecked at 1cm intervals in the appropriate state colours. The shoulder cord had a total width of 6.5cm and was placed upon a poppy red underlay which was not visible beyond the cords. Battalion number or monogram displayed.

Mecklenburg
As Prussia. Silver epaulette fields and crescents. Gilt battalion number. Epaulette braid: Silver with two carmine stripes. Shoulder cords: Silver flecked with blue and carmine silk with centre golden thread. Red cloth underlay.

Saxony
As Prussia. Silver epaulette fields. Crescents: JB12 and 13 silver. Schützen Regiment 108: Gilt. Battalion numbers corresponded. Epaulette braid: Silver with twc green stripes. Shoulder cords: Silver flecked with green silk. Hunting horn not displayed upon epaulettes or shoulder cords. Red cloth underlay.

Bavaria
As Prussia. Bright red (hochrot) epaulette fields. Gilt crescents. Epaulette braid: Silver with two light blue stripes. Shoulder cords: Silver flecked with light blue silk. Gilt Battalion numbers. Light green underlay.

3. UNDRESS TUNIC (Litewka)

Prussia
Of light grey cloth, doeskin or serge, the double-breasted Litewka was of a looser fit than the tunic but approximately of the same length. Possessing identical front sections, each cut together with the breast flaps of one piece, the coat displayed down the front two parallel rows, each of six domed gilt metal buttons. The buttons conformed to tunic size with the distance between the rows, upon the medium figure, from button centre to centre, about 16cm.

The collar was of a square-cut stand-or-fall pattern with slightly rounded lower front corners, piped in poppy red around the front and bottom edge with, adjoining the front piping each side of the collar, a rectangular patch 9.5cm long and 3.5cm wide. The patch was of dark green cloth for the Guard and Line Jäger, but of dark green velvet for the Guard Schützen; for both Guard battalions additionally piped red around all edges. Upon the rear of each patch a decorative 2.5cm diameter domed gilt button was displayed directly above and vertically in line with the shoulder button. In addition, poppy red piping extended down the tunic front and around each of the deep turn-back sleeve cuffs. A horizontal pocket flap without button was placed upon each front skirt while the rear skirt remained plain and undivided. The detachable shoulder cords were as on the tunic, upon a poppy red underlay.

Normally the Litewka was worn fully buttoned to the neck with a discreet amount of white shirt cuff revealed beneath the sleeves. The Litewka was strictly a casual garment worn only within defined military boundaries, such as the officers' mess, at the rifle range or at fencing, swimming or general sporting assemblies. It might also be called an interim tunic.

Mecklenburg
As Prussia. Light green collar patches, silver buttons.

Saxony
As Prussia. Dark green collar patches piped red around all outer edges. JB12 and 13: Silver buttons. Schützen Regiment 108: Gilt buttons.

Bavaria
Of individual pattern. Light green collar patches, gilt buttons.

4. TROUSERS AND FOOTWEAR (Hosen und Fussbekleidung)

Trousers (Hosen)

Prussia
The service trousers were basically of the men's pattern, but generally of a somewhat tighter cut and better material, such as tricot or satin. Long blue/black trousers were worn during the winter months, displaying down each outer seam a slightly narrower, 0.15cm, poppy red seam piping. The officer also retained a black leather stirrup strap attached to the base of each trouser leg passing beneath the arch of the shoe. The white linen summer trousers, without piping, also corresponded, with the stirrup strap of white cloth. Breeches, worn with the high stiff-shafted leather boot, were of blue/black tricot with 0.15cm poppy red seam piping, and for the mounted officer reinforced at the seat and each inner leg with black leather. For social occasions, gala trousers were worn, these as the long blue/black trousers, but of a much finer material, generally satin or cashmere, and displayed down each outer leg in addition to the narrow seam piping, two 3cm wide stripes of poppy red cloth, each spaced 0.5cm from the seam piping. The Guard Schützen substituted two 3cm stripes of black velvet, each additionally outlined on both sides with 0.2cm wide poppy red piping.

Mecklenburg
As Prussia. Gala trousers light green stripes, piped red each side.

Saxony
As Prussia.

Bavaria
As Prussia except light blue with light green piping for long cloth trousers and breeches. White trousers worn on parade.

Footwear (Fussbekleidung)

Prussia

The officers wore with the long blue/black or white trousers plain-fronted black leather shoes. The high stiff-shafted black leather boot, introduced in 1870 for the mounted and 1888 for the dismounted officers, extended to the base of the kneecap at the front arching to 4cm lower at the rear. Spurs were nickel plated or of polished steel and when worn with the high boot possessed an arched or upswept stem terminating in a smooth 2.2cm rowel. The spurs were attached to a broad black leather strap passing across the instep and in turn buckled to a narrower leather strap passing beneath the arch of the boot. With the long trousers the buckled spurs were replaced by box spurs, or the so-called 'dancing spurs' secured by a screwed fastening with a short straight neck terminating in a small, about 1cm diameter smooth button. In the field, high brown leather spirally strapped gaiters were adopted, extending to 5cm beneath the kneecap, and worn with brown leather laced ankle boots. Mounted officers with buckled spurs with brown leather straps. Later dark brown leather gaiters of a more elegant form were adopted, shaped to the leg and secured at the top by an adjustable buckled strap. Staff officers, adjutants and Captains customarily wore spurs with all orders of dress.

Mecklenburg, Saxony and Bavaria

In general corresponded to Prussia.

5. UNDRESS TOPCOAT, PARADE AND SERVICE TOPCOAT, GREATCOAT AND CAPE (Überrock, Paletot, Mantel mit Umhang)

Undress Topcoat (Überrock)

Prussia

A double-breasted frock coat of looser fit than the tunic and of dark green cloth, doeskin, or duffel, the Überrock was extremely popular with the officers. Revealing identical front sections, cut together with the breast flaps of one piece, the coat displayed two parallel rows each of six gilt metal buttons. The buttons were flat and 2.5cm in diameter, the lowest pair centred upon the waist seam, the remainder spaced equally above and vertically in line with the shoulder buttons. The stiff stand-up poppy red collar displayed a half-rounded front in all cases and the Jäger retained the narrow dark green piping around the front and upper edge. The Guard Schützen assumed a black velvet collar with red upper piping. The collar was without lace or embroidery with the fronts secured by two or three hooks and eyes, and a black silk neckband was just visible above.

The deep turn-back cuffs, the so-called 'cuff pockets', were of the same material as the coat and piped around the upper edge in poppy red. The back of the coat was made in two pieces revealing a vertical centre seam with the rear skirt divided into individual tails by a long vertical vent. The tail pocket flaps were straight, or rather tapered, that is wider at the base than at the top, each displaying two gilt buttons placed top and bottom, the uppermost pair centred on the rear waist seam, the lowest spaced 1.5cm above the base piping, the flaps further piped in poppy red. The coat was considerably shorter than the Paletot, reaching only to the centre of the kneecaps.

Shoulder cords were as on the tunic mounted on a poppy red underlay and epaulettes and epaulette bridles were no longer displayed upon the Überrock. The breast flaps were generally lined in the same material as the tunic collar, that is of poppy red cloth, but dark green velvet for the Guard Schützen, though normally the coat was worn fully buttoned to the neck and this was not revealed.

The Überrock was frequently worn on manoeuvres, Adjutants with the sash 'en bandoulière', military umpires and other judiciaries wore a white brassard around the left upper arm. Hooks and eyes were sewn into each front and rear skirt enabling them to be attached together giving greater leg freedom when mounted, etc., and also revealing the black linings. For informal occasions the Überrock was worn with either the long blue/black trousers or, in summer, white linen, with black leather shoes. In the field the high-shafted black leather boot was worn with spurs where permitted. Ensigns were permitted to wear the Überrock with the shoulder straps of the men.

Mecklenburg
As Prussia with light green collar piped red around all outer edges. Breast flap linings light green, buttons silver.

Saxony
As Prussia with black velvet collar piped red around all outer edges. Breast flap linings black velvet, buttons silver for Jäger, gilt for Schützen Regiment 108.

Bavaria
As Prussia except of light blue material with two rows, each of seven buttons down the front. Collar light green piped light blue around front and upper edge. Light green piping down the front and around each sleeve cuff. Breast flap linings light green, buttons gilt. Tail pocket flaps piped light green.

Parade and Service Topcoat (Paletot)

Prussia
A most stylish, yet practical, double-breasted topcoat and made of a variety of materials, the Paletot adopted an extremely light shade of grey, ranging almost to the point of white. The coat displayed down the front two parallel rows, each of six domed gilt buttons, the lowest pair centred 5cm beneath the hips, 20–24cm apart, the rest spaced equally above in line with the shoulder buttons.

The deep square-fronted collar provided with three pairs of hooks and eyes and of a stand-and-fall pattern, displayed, when reclined or 'nach innen', the dark green colour of the tunic and, when raised or 'nach aussen', the colour of the tunic collar, in the case of the Guard and Line Jäger of poppy red cloth, but for the Guard Schützen of black velvet with poppy red piping. An appropriately coloured cloth or velvet tab with button was also provided to retain the collar in its raised position.

Sleeve cuffs were of a deep turn-back pattern and of the same material as the coat and, upon each front skirt, a sloping pocket flap without button was placed, its highest point in line with the lowest front button.

The back of the coat revealed a long vertical pleat, stitched in a quilted triangle at the top, extending down to the base of the half-belt formed of two short straps of equal length secured at the centre by a single domed gilt metal button. At each end of the half-belt was a vertical arched pocket flap displaying a row of three domed gilt metal buttons, and further outlined with 0.2cm poppy red piping. The divided rear skirt could be closed by four small grey cloth-covered buttons provided on the inner left-hand side. Always worn fastened when dismounted.

The small domed gilt shoulder buttons securing the upper ends of the shoulder cords remained unobscured when the collar was folded and were in all respects as on the tunic. Epaulettes were not worn. Considerable discretion was permitted in the length of the coat and while the regulations stipulated 24cm above the instep, it was also worn well above or well below the kneecaps, but always remained shorter than the Mantel.

In the field the Paletot was carried rolled in horseshoe fashion around the three outer edges of the pack. If the pack was not carried, then 'en bandoulière' from the left shoulder or, by the mounted officer, rolled within a light grey valise strapped behind the saddle.

The Paletot on all parade and service occasions was worn fully buttoned to the neck, only officers of General status were permitted to leave the top two buttons unfastened with the breast flaps turned back to reveal the linings.

Mecklenburg
As Prussia. Collar reclined dark green, collar raised poppy red. Silver domed buttons.

Saxony
As Prussia. Collar reclined dark green, collar raised black velvet piped red. Jäger: Silver domed buttons. Schützen Regiment 108: Gilt.

Bavaria
As Prussia. Collar reclined light blue, collar raised light green. Rear waist belt of one piece, attached to upper pocket flap buttons only. Divided rear skirt fastened by small gilt metal buttons.

Officers' Greatcoat with Cape (Mantel mit Umhang)

Prussia
The Mantel was worn only on undress or off-duty occasions, or in the field by the mounted officer. A single-breasted garment of light grey cloth, in reality much darker than the Paletot, the coat fastened at the front by six gilt domed metal buttons, the lowest button 1cm above the waist. The back section of the coat revealed a double pleat stitched together at the collar seam, and the rear skirt was divided by a long vertical vent which could be fastened by four small cloth buttons provided on the left-hand side.

The square-cut, stand-and-fall collar, as for the Paletot, in its folded position was dark green and, when raised, poppy red or, for the Guard Schützen, of black velvet with red piping. When raised the collar covered the ears, not merely the neck as the Paletot. The Mantel at its minimum length conformed to the longest Paletot, but generally extended to 5cm above the ankles. In all other respects, that is sleeves, tail pocket flaps, rear waist belt, etc, conformed to the Paletot. Shoulder cords were not displayed.

A Pelerine or shoulder-cape, without sleeves or armholes, of the same light grey material, was permanently attached beneath the coat collar. The cape was made in two pieces with a vertical back seam and, with the arms vertically at the sides, the base of the cape hung level with the extended finger tips.

Mecklenburg and Saxony
As Prussia.

Bavaria
As Prussia except Pelerine attached by small gilt buttons.

Officers' Cape and Hood (Umhang und Kapuze)

Prussia
Introduced in 1899, of light grey waterproofed cloth or rubberised fabric lined with grey silk, the officers' cape was much longer than the Pelerine, extending to well below the knee. The cape was fastened at the front by five concealed bone buttons covered in the same material, and possessed a deep square-cut collar conforming in all respects to that of the Mantel. On the inside of the cape, at waist height, a buttonhole flap was provided enabling the cape to be secured to the rear waist buttons of the tunic or Paletot in high wind. The circular cape, made of two parts with a vertical back seam, hung in loose deep folds, but was without any external pockets and displayed no rank insignia upon the shoulders. The provision of a neck halter stitched to the inner collar band, as with the Paletot, was optional. The cape was worn either alone or above the Paletot, but in the field was strapped around the outer edges of the pack above the Paletot, or, if pack not carried, 'en bandoulière' from the left shoulder.

A row of small grey cloth-covered buttons was provided above the base of the collar seam, both on the inside and outside, to which, in the field, was attached a light grey hood with poppy red lining. Normally the hood was attached to the inside buttons but in heavy rain was re-buttoned to the outside to cover the raised cape collar. When not raised the hood was suspended in a flat manner, revealing its poppy red lining, from beneath the cape collar. The hood, of the same material as the cape, possessed a circular crown-piece of lighter grey silk or calico, not visible when the shako was worn.

Mecklenburg, Saxony and Bavaria
As Prussia

6. BODY SASH, ADJUTANTS' SASH, UNDRESS SERVICE BELT (Leib-Schärpe, Adjutantenschärpe, Feldbinde)

Body Sash (Leib-Schärpe)

Prussia
Displayed in the heraldic colours of the Hohenzollerns, the waist, or body sash was composed of silver cords laced with two 0.5cm wide black silk stripes, each spaced 1cm from the outer edges. At the front the sash rested upon the lowest front tunic button and, at the rear, upon the uppermost button pair of the tail pocket flaps. The sash was retained in a bow at the left hip by two adjustable silver plated buckles, the suspended ends each terminating in silver bell-rope tassels. The bright silver tassel crowns were contrasted with an outer net of dull

silver, while the 25–30cm long tassels were composed of two outer rows of silver fringes with an inner filling of mixed black and silver fringes.

For the dismounted officer the base of the rear tassel was adjusted level with the left knee joint, with the front tassel higher by the depth of its crown. When mounted the tassels remained in this position, but for convenience were adjusted some 10cm higher. The sash was worn only on parade or ceremonial occasions.

Mecklenburg
Golden sash pierced with two silk stripes, the upper blue, the lower carmine. Golden tassels composed of two outer rows of golden fringes with an inner filling of mixed dark blue and carmine fringes. Gilt adjustable buckles and lined with yellow silk.

Saxony
Silver sash laced with two green stripes. Crown as Prussia. Silver tassels composed of two outer rows of silver fringes with an inner filling of mixed silver and green fringes.

Bavaria
Silver sash pierced with two light blue stripes. Silver tassels with spherical crowns and bulbous stems resembling in shape those of the men's sabre knot. Tassels composed of two outer rows of silver fringes with an inner filling of mixed light blue and silver fringes.

Adjutants' Sash (Adjutantenschärpe)

Prussia
The silver adjutants' sash, introduced in 1848, and an article of normal service dress, was worn 'en bandoulière' from the right shoulder to the left hip, passing beneath the epaulette or shoulder cord, and terminating in silver bullion tassels of the same dimensions and displayed in the same position as on the waist sash. The sash band, 6–7cm wide, was laced with two parallel black silk stripes, each about 0.9cm wide, spaced 1.5cm from the outer edges. The sash was formed into a wrapped tie at the left hip and retained in position by two small loops of silver cord, the upper loop attached to the right shoulder button, the lower to the left rear waist button. The sash was generally lined with white silk.

Mecklenburg
As body sash, golden with an upper blue and lower carmine stripe. The retaining loops of golden cord.

Saxony
As body sash, silver with two green stripes.

Bavaria
As body sash, silver pierced with two light blue stripes.

Undress Service Belt or Waist Belt (Feldbinde)

Prussia
Composed of silver cords, as the sash band, but stiffened with a cloth or velvet backing, the service belt displayed two 0.5cm wide black silk stripes, each spaced 1cm from the outer edges. The gilt circular buckle was embossed in the centre with the crowned monogram WII enclosed within a laurel leaf wreath.

Each side of the buckle a vertical slide of narrower sash band was displayed, each 2.2cm wide with two 0.3cm black silk stripes. When worn with the tunic the Feldbinde obscured the lowest front button and at the rear rested upon the waist buttons.

In the field or on manoeuvres the Feldbinde was often replaced, in particular by the staff officers, by a 2–4cm wide black leather strap buckled around the waist to which the black leather binocular case was also attached.

Mecklenburg
Silver band pierced with two silk stripes, the upper dark blue, the lower of carmine with, in the centre, a narrower golden thread. Slides corresponded. The blue and carmine stripes, each 0.5cm wide; on the slides 0.3cm, with the golden thread respectively 0.2 and 0.1cm wide. Silver-plated buckle bearing crowned monogram FF within a laurel leaf wreath.

Saxony
Silver band with two green stripes. Slides corresponded. Buckle silver for Jäger, gilt for Schützen Regiment 108, bearing crowned monogram FA within laurel leaf wreath.

Bavaria
Silver band pierced with two light blue stripes. Slides corresponded. Gilt buckle bearing royal Bavarian crown within laurel leaf wreath.

7. SWORDS AND SWORDKNOTS (Degen und Portepée)

Officers' Sword (Degen)

Prussia
The Jäger officer carried the infantry pattern '89 sword. This possessed a gilt basket hilt embodying the crowned heraldic Prussian eagle, with the grip, slightly inclined to the front, covered in black sharkskin and wrapped at each knuckle-join with twisted silver wire. On the outer side of the grip the Guard displayed the silver eight-pointed Guard star with enamelled centre, and the Line the gilt crowned monogram WRII. The sword was carried in a blackened steel scabbard with a single silver-plated suspension ring and was protected at the base by a flat, roughly pear-shaped metal drag. The sword had a total length varying between 84.5cm–104cm.

The sword belt, worn around the waist beneath the tunic, was of red Russia leather or webbing material with, attached on the left-hand side, a brown leather frog from which was suspended the long leather sling and a short brass hook or blackened snap safety clip permitting the sword to be carried either on a long or short drag. The sword sling of red Morocco or red Russia leather was faced with a 2cm wide plain golden braid for the Guard or silver for the Line, with a narrow strip of the basic leather remaining visible each side of the braid. The sling was adjusted by a gilt rectangular spiked buckle, its pointed end attached to the scabbard ring by means of a metal snap safety hook provided on the inner side.

Mecklenburg
Pattern '89 sword carried on parade and service occasions. Gilt basket hilt bearing crowned state coat of arms with star of the Wendish crown upon the grip. Sword sling of Morocco leather faced with plain golden braid. On undress occasions the old curved Jäger sabre was carried, with gilt stirrup hilt bearing griffin's head, in natural steel scabbard. Grip decorated with gilt crowned monogram FF enclosed within a silver oak leaf wreath.

Saxony
Similar to '89 pattern, but of Saxon form. Gilt stirrup basket hilt bearing inverted crowned state coat of arms within elaborate filigree. Grip without device. Sword sling red Morocco leather faced with plain silver braid.

Bavaria
Infantry officers' sabre carried with plain gilt stirrup hilt. Blade slightly curved. Sword sling of light green Morocco leather faced with plain silver braid with light blue silk centre stripe provided with two rectangular silver-plated adjustable buckles.

The Swordknot (Portepée)

Prussia
Ranking, together with the body sash, as the true insignia of the officer, the swordknot was tied to the hilt of the sword, passed around the grip and draped over the basket guard, with the acorn suspended to the front. Of universal pattern for all officers of the army and since 1896 based on the cavalry pattern, this represented a black Morocco leather strap interlaced each side and in the centre with a narrow silver metallic thread. The slide was also basically of black leather, interlaced with silver threads and the flattish, barrel-shaped silver stem additionally wrapped with bright silver net. The crown was composed of twisted silver cords laid horizontally, with the acorn formed of vertical twisted silver cords with an inner core of mixed black and silver fringes.

Mecklenburg
Strap of black Morocco leather interlaced each side and in the centre with a narrow golden metallic thread. Black leather slide interlaced with golden thread, stem wrapped with gilt net. Crown of horizontal gilt cords, acorn of gilt vertical cords with inner core of mixed blue/carmine/gold fringes.

Saxony
Strap of black Morocco leather interlaced each side with a silver thread and in the centre with a silver/green/silver thread. Slide of black leather interlaced with silver and green threads, with abbreviated stem and crown of silver. Large acorn of silver cords with inner core of mixed silver/green fringes.

Bavaria
Resembled the sabreknot of the men in form. Strap of light green Morocco leather faced with silver braid and edged each side with two light blue silk stripes. The spherical slide and bulbous stem interwoven silver and light blue with crown of horizontal silver cords upon a light blue velvet underlay. Acorn of silver cords with inner core of mixed silver/light blue fringes. On undress occasions, a less ornate interim pattern of portepée was carried, suspended from the strap by a silver-plated ring.

8. PARADE AND SERVICE SADDLE CLOTH (Paradeüberlegedecke und Satteluntderdecke)

Parade Saddle Cloth (Paradeüberlegedecke)

Prussia
The Überlegedecke was draped over the saddle and corresponded to the dark green colour of the tunic, trimmed around all outer edges with two parallel golden metallic braids. The inner, narrower, braid was spaced 1cm above the outer, wider, braid, with a narrow strip of the basic dark green cloth remaining visible beyond this. All four corners of the rectangular cloth were rounded, with a decorative golden metallic or embroidered ornament diagonally displayed in each hind corner. For the Guard Jäger and Guard Schützen this took the form of the silver eight-pointed Guard star with a golden yellow, almost orange, centre field displaying the black Old Prussian eagle. The Line displayed, either in gold metal or embroidery, the gilt crowned monogram FWR. On parade the sword was not attached to the saddle cloth but always suspended from the rider's waist and the parade cloth was only displayed by staff officers and adjutants. Captains retained the service cloth.

Mecklenburg
As Prussia. Inner and outer braid trim of silver. In each hind corner silver crowned monogram FF.

Saxony
Rectangular dark green cloth with, for Captains and adjutants, wide black velvet stripe additionally piped red each side. For staff officers an additional narrow black velvet stripe piped red each side spaced 1cm above.

Bavaria
Parade saddle cloth discontinued 1910. Light blue service saddle cloth generally utilised on all occasions.

Service Saddle Cloth (Satteluntderdecke or Dienstdecke)

Prussia
Worn beneath the saddle and of a thick, fine quality, blanket felt termed 'Eskimo', the interim or undress saddle cloth remained of the same dark blue as the infantry's, with the exception of the Guard Jäger's of dark green. Rectangular in shape, but possessing rounded front corners, an integral cloth map pocket with cloth buttoned arched flap was provided on the right-hand side with, on the left, a protective black leather pad, about 25cm long, to protect against the chafing of the sword. At the front, across the withers, a protective crescent-shaped piece of soft black leather was set into the cloth.

The saddle cloth, laid beneath the saddle in such a manner that an equal 8cm of the cloth remained visible both to the front and rear, was completely plain without trim or ornament. A brown leather sword holster supported by two adjustable leather straps was secured to the saddle behind the rider's left thigh. Service Saddle cloth was carried by all mounted officers including Captains.

In the field, the undress saddle cloth was often replaced by a large greyish-brown saddle blanket, 234cm long and 200cm wide, folded in four beneath the saddle.

Mecklenburg and Saxony
As Prussia.

Bavaria
As Prussia, except light blue cloth.

9. EFFECTS (Effekten)

Officers' Pack (Tornister)

Prussia
The officers' pack, entirely of black patent leather and slightly smaller than the men's, was carried only by the dismounted officer. The black leather shoulder straps, each passing under the shoulder cords or over the epaulette straps, were of the same pattern as the men's, tapering from 4.4cm at the top to 2cm at the base, but attached directly to the base of the pack without the narrow support straps.

The pack flap was secured by three adjustably buckled black leather straps, and additional black leather buckled straps, one on top and one on each lower side of the pack, served to attach the rolled Paletot, Cape, etc. All attached metal fittings of brass. Staff officers did not carry the pack nor, from 1888, did the Captains, the practice only being continued by the dismounted Lieutenants.

Mecklenburg
As Prussia.

Saxony
As Prussia.

Bavaria
As infantry, basically of dark brown leather covered with reddish-brown calf-hide with black leather support straps.

Map Case (Kartentasche)

The black patent leather map case with rounded base corners was provided with an overlapping flap optionally fastened in the centre by a buttoned or buckled leather strap. The case was originally suspended from the left-hand, later the right-hand, side of the sword belt beneath the tunic by three black leather straps which were attached to brass rings provided on rear walls. In the field it was carried by an adjustable black leather strap, attached to the side walls, from the left shoulder to the right hip, or by staff officers and adjutants looped by two or three black leather straps from the right-hand side of the narrow waist strap.

Binoculars (Doppelfernglas)

Contained in a black leather case looped to the right-hand side of the waist belt, the hinged lid fastened at the front by a buttoned leather strap. For convenience the binoculars were often removed from the case and slung around the neck. For NCOs the lid of the binocular case was hinged at the front and secured by straps to the side walls, in the manner of the ammunition pouch, with a rectangular brass buckle provided upon the case enabling the pack strap to be attached, if necessary. German binoculars, as all optical equipment, were of a very high standard and generally of Zeiss manufacture.

Gloves (Handschuhe)

For service wear and general duties of reddish-brown leather, but for parade, church going and social occasions white leather was substituted. The gloves were normally fastened by one or two buttons or press studs covered in the same material, and possessed distinctly ribbed backs.

Whistle Lanyard (Signalpfeife-schnur)

Adopted only in the field, the signal whistle was carried on a dark green plaited cord looped between the second and third front tunic or topcoat buttons. Carried by all company officers, but in particular the Lieutenants.

Pistol Holster (Pistolentasche)

Looped to the left-hand side of the Feldbinde with the pistol butt presented to the right, the holster was of dark brown leather secured by an adjustable buckled flap. Adjutants carried the holster on the narrow black leather waist strap. Various patterns of automatic pistol were carried, the most common the Mauser 7.92mm calibre and the Parabellum '08 9mm calibre, the latter containing the ammunition clip within the butt. In addition to the officers, those NCOs not armed with the rifle, for example the Feldwebel, Vizefeldwebel, Colour-bearer and Music Master, also carried the pistol.

10. HEAD-DRESS (Kopfbedeckung)

Shako (Tschako)

Prussia

Basically of black lacquered leather with both front and rear peaks, the body of the shako, between the raised leather brii im and the 2.5cm wide leather baseband, was entirely covered with black cloth with a silvered ventilation grille provided on each upper side. The flat gilt metal chinscales were secured each side by circular gilt rosettes with, beneath the right-hand rosette, the 'Deutsche' or imperial black/silver/red cockade, about 5.5cm in diameter, with its inner red field distinctly revealed.

The shako plate for the Guard was the silver-plated Guard star with enamelled centre field, displaying around the outer points of the star a silver circular scroll bearing the inscription 'MIT GOTT FÜR KOENIG UND VATERLAND' and at the base the commemorative date '1860'.

Officers of the Line Battalions 1, 2, 5 and 6 adopted the old gilt 'Grenadier' eagle bearing upon its oval breastshield the entwined monogram FWR. The remaining battalions displayed the customary gilt Line eagle with the breast initials FR and both patterns of eagle displayed the Fatherland scroll across the breast and wings. JB10 was singularly distinguished by the addition to the eagle of a gilt circular scroll bearing the battle honours 'Waterloo/Peninsula/Venta del Pozo'.

The elliptical fieldbadge, half extending above the shako and secured by a silver-plated wire stem, displayed an outer border of brilliant silver metallic cords, and an inner field of black velvet additionally enclosed within an oval silver metallic cord. The officers of JB7 retained the silver/blue/red fieldbadge of Schaumburg-Lippe, the outer border of silver cords, the inner field of dark blue velvet, enclosed within an oval red enamelled cord.

On parade the officers displayed black buffalo-hair plumes, the base of the plume level with the upper seam of the front peak. The plume, supported on a gilt fluted funnel slightly inclined to the front, was secured at the top by a gilt retainer button. In the field a grey-green linen shako cover without number was worn, clipped to the front and rear peaks, with only the fieldbadge displayed. On manoeuvres umpires wore a white shako cover, the officers of the 'red party' a red band around the base of the grey-green linen cover.

Officers of the Reserve were distinguished by the Landwehr Cross upon the plate, resembling a Maltese Cross in form and generally displayed in silver, only reversing to gilt upon the silver plates. As the Cross itself carried the inscription 'MIT GOTT FUR KOENIG UND VATERLAND 1813', the customary Fatherland scroll was rendered superfluous and not adopted. Guard Reserve officers displayed the gilt Cross superimposed on the top ray of the Guard star, its base resting upon the circular scroll bearing the inscription 'SUUM CUIQUE'. Line Reserve officers displayed the silver cross immediately beneath the monogram FWR or initials FR upon the breast of the eagle. Reserve officers of JB10 retained the Battle Honour Scroll.

Generals à la suite displayed the cock-feather plume of the infantry General, for Prussia the outer feathers in white, the inner of black.

Mecklenburg

As Prussia. Shako plate displaying twelve-rayed gilt heraldic sun with abbreviated base, bearing the silver crowned coat of arms enclosed within a laurel leaf wreath. Fieldbadge: Outer border of silver cords, inner velvet field quartered dark blue and carmine by a golden cross and further outlined with golden cord. Gilt chinscales with black buffalo-hair plumes.

Reserve Officers: Silver Landwehr Cross bearing inscription 'MIT GOTT FUR FUERST UND VATERLAND'.

Saxony

Shako in the form of a Keppi without rear peak. Black leather chinstrap with rosettes in button colour. Beneath the right-hand rosette the imperial black/silver/red cockade, beneath the left the Saxon white/green/white. The outer rim of the Saxon cockades was smooth not 'cockscombed' as the Prussian, and a fieldbadge was not displayed. Officers of Battalions 12 and 13 displayed a silver eight-pointed star bearing the gilt crowned coat of arms with hunting horn at the base. By Schützen Regiment 108 the colours were reversed. Black buffalo-hair plumes bound in the form of a bow and retained by a small black leather buckled strap were displayed on all service occasions on the left-hand side of the shako. The shako was covered with black velveteen with, around the crown, a black velvet band upon which the staff officers displayed three, the company officers two rings of silver embroidery. Schützen Regiment 108 substituted golden embroidery.

Reserve Officers: Landwehr Cross superimposed on base of star, its upper arm immediately beneath the centre field. Gilt cross for JB12 and 13. Silver for Schützen Regiment 108. Generals à la suite: Customary black shako plume retained.

Bavaria
As Prussia. Shako plate: Gilt crowned coat of arms with crowned lion supporters mounted upon a scroll bearing the inscription 'IN TREUE FEST'. Gilt metal fittings and flat chinscales with, beneath the right chinscale rosette, the imperial black/silver/red cockade. Fieldbadge with outer border of silver cords, inner field of light blue velvet enclosed within a twisted silver metallic cord. Shako plumes not displayed.

Reserve Officers: Silver Landwehr cross bearing light blue/silver diamond patterned shield superimposed on state coat of arms. Generals a la suite: Cockfeather shako plume, outer white, inner light blue.

Service Cap (Mütze)

Prussia
The service cap of the officer was of a higher and stiffer construction than the men's, of finer material such as duffel or felt, and additionally possessed a rounded black patent leather peak with bound edge angled between 30–35 degrees. The front and side walls of the cap were retained at an equal height by flexible stiffeners, outwardly slanting up to the crown. A chinstrap was not adopted. The cockades, each 2cm in diameter, were also of much better quality, the outer cockscombed base of lacquered leather bearing in the centre a distinctively raised gilt or silver metal ring with recessed inner field of cloth or velvet. The capband, deeper than the men's, 3.9cm including pipings, corresponded in colour, with all cap pipings similarly 0.2cm wide. A narrow strip of the basic cap material always remained visible beneath the base of the capband. Measured vertically across the cockades from the base of the capband to the upper crown piping, the cap officially had a height of 8.5cm, with the crown about 5.2cm wider than the diameter of the headband. Additional distinctions:

(a) Reserve Officers: Distinguished by a miniature silver Landwehr Cross displayed within the centre of the state cockade.

(b) Guard Jäger and Line Battalions 1–11: Dark green crown cloth, poppy red capband with red crown piping. Upper cockade: Black/silver/red. Lower cockade: Black/silver/black.

(c) Guard Schützen: Dark green crown cloth, black velvet capband piped poppy red top and bottom, with red crown piping. Upper cockade: Black/silver/red. Lower cockade: Black/silver/black.

(d) Officers of Jäger Battalion 7: Lower cockade: Silver/red/silver.

Mecklenburg
Dark green crown cloth, light green capband piped red top and bottom, red crown piping. Upper cockade: Black/silver/red. Lower cockade: Blue/gold/carmine.

Reserve officers: Gilt Landwehr cross within state cockade.

Saxony
Dark green crown cloth, black velvet capband piped red top and bottom with red crown piping. Upper cockade: Black/silver/red. Lower cockade: Silver/green/silver.

Reserve officers JB12 and 13: Gilt Landwehr cross. Schützen Regiment 108: Silver Landwehr cross within state cockade.

Bavaria
Light blue crown cloth, light green capband with light green crown piping. Upper cockade: Black/silver/red. Lower cockade: Silver/light blue/silver.

Reserve officers: Silver Landwehr cross bearing light blue/silver diamond patterned shield within state cockade.

COLLAR BUTTONS

Prussia

Mecklenburg

Saxony

Bavaria

EPAULETTES

Oberleutnant
Major

Hauptmann
Oberstleutnant

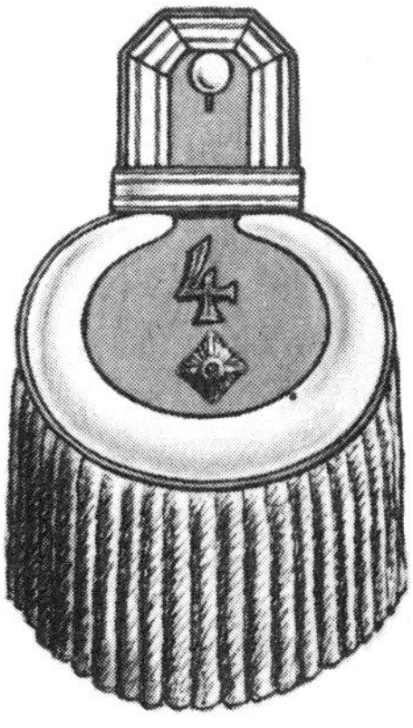

Leutnant

SECTION III

The Field Service Dress – Officers & Men

1. THE FIELD TUNIC (Feldwaffenrock)

Prussia

(a) NCOs and men: The 1910-adopted field or manoeuvre uniform imposed a totally different appearance upon the Jäger. From this period on the Jäger, as indeed the entire army, possessed two completely distinct uniforms, the old dark green retained for peacetime service and the new grey-green devised specifically for war.

The field tunic entirely of grey-green cloth remained single-breasted and fastened by a vertical row of eight buttons, but differed from the peacetime tunic in that the front sections, including skirts, were cut entirely from one piece with only the back section divided from the skirt by a rear waist seam. In addition, a sloping pocket flap was provided on each front skirt, secured by a small tombac button embossed with the royal Prussian crown. The arched tail pocket flaps were traditionally retained one each side of the divided rear skirt, displaying the customary six buttons arranged as three horizontal pairs. The uppermost pair remained in the form of button-hooks, with additional belt support provided at each hip by a tombac suspender hook.

The tunic buttons were of domed pattern and peacetime dimension, but of a dark or matt tombac, each with a smooth raised outer rim and, with the exception of the small shoulder buttons, embossed with the Prussian crown upon a pebbled background. The shoulder buttons, reduced to 1.8cm diameter, retained the customary Arabic company number from 1–6.

The collar, of a re-styled stand-and-fall pattern with somewhat rounded lower front corners, was piped light green around the front and lower edge for both Guard and Line Jäger and black for the Guard Schützen. The Guard Jäger displayed their elongated yellow double lace with light green inner lights, the Guard Schützen with black. In all cases a grey-green cloth tab and grey button were provided on the inner side of the collar, as on the Litewka, to retain the collar in a raised position. Beneath the collar a field grey cotton neck cloth was universally worn, fashioned at the front in the manner of a cravat and somewhat more revealed than in peacetime.

Light green tunic piping replaced the peacetime poppy red, remaining 0.2cm wide and extending the full length of the tunic front and outlining each of the arched tail pocket flaps. The pointed grey-green shoulder straps were similarly piped around all outer edges in light green and reduced to 5.5cm wide, including piping, and universally displaying the battalion number or monogram in red. The shoulder straps were rendered detachable and provided with a grey-green cloth loop at each upper armhole seam through which the base tongue of the strap passed. The shoulder straps of the Guard remained without insignia.

Sleeve cuffs conformed to peacetime pattern, the Swedish with two horizontally-in-line crown buttons, or the French with a vertical row of three crown buttons, no longer revealing coloured facings but instead the basic grey-green tunic material. The Swedish was outlined in light green piping around the upper and rear edge, the French in black, around the cuff and the rear edges of the patch, while the Guard was additionally distinguished by a piping around the base edge. Both cuff patterns retained the 13cm long rear seam slit adjustably fastened by a grey-green cloth tab and button and JB10 its light blue 'Gibraltar' sleeve band 8cm above the cuff. All cuff lace remained of yellow linen and peacetime dimension, but with light green inner lights for the Guard Jäger and black for the Guard Schützen.

(b) Bandsmen and Musicians: The signal-buglers customarily remained without swallows' nests, but the NCO musicians or 'Waldhornisten' retained swallows' nests of peacetime form, but basically of grey-green cloth and, if no fringe displayed, piped along the base in light green. Golden metallic Oberjäger braid, plain or patterned as in peacetime, the Guard with 3cm long thin golden fringes, the Music Master of both Guard and Line with 7cm long silver fringes.

(c) Music Masters: Tunic of officer cut but in the case of the Guard without the officers' collar patches but instead the elongated lace pattern of the men except of silver-grey silk with light green or black inner lights. The Music Master swallows' nests became grey-green with eight silver pointed braids each laced with two black silk stripes and with silver fringes as in peacetime. The sash-girdle now of grey-green cloth, together with its slides, was bordered each side with a dull silver-grey silk stripe, each laced with two black silk stripes, with both the belt and slides additionally piped around the edges in light green. The gilt circular buckle remained as in peacetime and the universal poppy red shoulder cords with metal lyre and battalion number or monogram were unchanged.

(d) Officers: The grey-green tunic of the officer retained its two-piece back section and better cut and material with the preference for varying grades of doeskin. Fastened at the front by a row of eight crown buttons, with light green piping down the front and around each tail pocket flap, the tunic remained of peacetime length with the skirts lined with grey-green silk. Metal suspender hooks were additionally positioned one each side of the waist and an inner map pocket optionally provided inside the left-hand front skirt. A grey-green stand-and-fall collar was adopted maintaining its distinctly higher form, though not exceeding a stand of 5cm and a fall of 6cm. The collar, with rounded lower corners, was secured by only two hooks and eyes, piped around the front and lower edge in light green for both Guard and Line Jäger and black velvet for the Guard Schützen. For the Line, the collar remained plain, but the Guard replaced their peacetime golden embroidery with coloured rectangular patches, 4.3cm wide and 7.5cm long, each adjoining the collar piping at the front and displaying an abbreviated double Kapellen lace of a matt silver-grey weave. The patch for

OFFICERS' BELT BUCKLES

Prussia Mecklenburg Saxony Bavaria

the Guard Jäger was of light green cloth, that of the Guard Schützen of dark green velvet, both additionally piped red around all outer edges. The upper and lower inner lights of the lace each revealed a narrow 0.3cm silver twisted cord with only the centre dart displaying the base colour of the patch with the lace spaced an equal 0.2cm from the front and rear edge of the patch. Beneath the collar a grey silk neck cloth was worn rather more revealed than in peacetime.

Sleeve cuffs remained of the Swedish or French pattern, no longer with coloured facings, but adopting the grey-green colour of the tunic and outlined with light green piping, or black velvet for the Guard Schützen, Guard officers with the additional piping around the base of the cuff. The Guard adopted a cuff lace of a dull silver-grey weave, the inner light replaced by silver twisted cord, arranged as two vertical laces upon the Swedish or three horizontal laces upon the French patch. The matt gilt tunic buttons were each, including the small shoulder buttons, embossed with the royal Prussian crown. A sloping pocket flap, with rounded front corners but without button, was placed on each front skirt, positioned somewhat more diagonally and further forward than the men's, and concealed an arched pocket entry.

Shoulder cords remained as in peacetime upon a poppy red underlay, later assuming a matt, not bright, finish with the shoulder button reduced to 1.8cm diameter and epaulette bridles were dispensed with. Rank insignia was unaltered but the newly-established rank of Feldwebel-Leutnant or Sergeant-Major Lieutenant wore the uniform of the officer with the shoulder cords of a Leutnant and the collar and cuff braid and large eagle button of the Feldwebel. All other dress effects were as the officer and the rank was included within the officer corps.

Mecklenburg (JB14)

As Prussia. White collar and cuff lace with light green inner lights. All tunic pipings light green. Red number 14 on pointed shoulder straps. Dull nickel crown buttons and silver NCO braid and collar buttons. Swallows' nests with 3cm silver fringes. Music Master braid: Silver-grey with two carmine stripes.

Officers light green collar patches piped poppy red with abbreviated dull silver lace. Shoulder cords as peacetime. Matt silver crown buttons.

Saxony (JB12, 13 & Schützen Regiment 108)

As Prussia, but retained the Saxon peculiarities of the German cuff, straight tail pocket flaps, and base skirt piping, but adopted the pointed Prussian shoulder straps. All tunic pipings light green. Battalion numbers and hunting horn upon the shoulder straps red. Jäger Battalion 12 and 13 dull nickel crown buttons. Silver NCO braid and collar buttons. Schützen Regiment 108 collar and cuffs piped black. Matt tombac crown buttons. Remaining pipings light green. Golden NCO braid and collar buttons. Music Master braid: Silver-grey with two green stripes. Officers' shoulder cords as in peacetime.

Bavaria (JB1 & 2)

As Prussia, but of field grey cloth. Light green battalion numbers upon the field grey shoulder straps. All tunic pipings light green. Matt tombac buttons embossed with crowned Bavarian lion. Golden NCO braid and collar buttons. All badge insignia on field grey underlay. Music Master braid: Silver-grey with two light blue stripes. Waist girdle field grey. Officers' shoulder cords as in peacetime.

2. NCO RANK INSIGNIA (Unteroffizierdienstgradabzeichen)

The system of indicating NCO rank remained fundamentally unchanged but, due to the refashioned collar, the golden metallic braid, reduced to 1.6cm wide, was re-positioned around the front and base edge, applied in a square-cut manner for both Guard and Line. The Guard retained patterned braid, the Line plain, and the eagle collar buttons remained unchanged except now of dull tombac or nickel. The Guard Oberjäger retained the single yellow collar lace with the front chaplet slightly overlapped by the braid.

Upon both patterns of cuff the rank braid remained basically unaltered, spaced 0.2cm from the outer piping but terminating about 0.3cm from the base of the cuff.

The rank of Offizierstellvetreter or acting officer introduced upon mobilisation, adopted the collar and cuff braid of the Vizefeldwebel with, in addition, a golden 1.6cm wide metallic braid around the outer edges of the pointed shoulder straps spaced 0.1cm from the piping, patterned for the Guard, and plain for the Line. A gilt metal battalion number or monogram of company officer size was displayed upon the centre of the strap and the officers' sword and sword-knot was carried. Ranked as a Senior NCO, not an officer.

3. SERVICE GRADE INSIGNIA (Dienststellungsabzeichen)

All peacetime service grade insignia, such as that of the One-Year Volunteer and Re-enlisted man, was retained upon the field tunic except that the Colour-bearers', signallers' and medical badge were placed on a grey-green cloth underlay and the eagle marksmanship buttons assumed a dull tombac. The Emperor's badge continued to be displayed on a grey-green backing and marksmanship cords were worn. Medical personnel retained the Red Cross brassard on the left upper arm, assistant stretcher-bearers an entirely red arm band.

4. FIELD TROUSERS (Feldhosen)

Prussia

As the tunic, of grey-green cloth with 0.2cm light green seam piping and cut in the fashion of breeches or 'Stiefelhosen'. Worn with the leather marching boots which were left in their natural tan brown condition. Officers adopted Stiefelhosen of grey-green tricot with light green seam piping worn with dark brown leggings and brown leather ankle boots laced at the front. Mounted officers with brown leather buckled spurs of peacetime pattern. Long grey-green trousers with light green seam piping were also worn with black shoes. Mecklenburg and Saxony corresponded to Prussia, but Bavaria adopted field grey trousers with light green piping.

Mecklenburg
As Prussia

Saxony
As Prussia

Bavaria
Field grey trousers with light green piping.

5. GREATCOAT (Mantel)

Remained as peacetime with poppy red patches, but with the substitution of grey-green shoulder straps piped light green with red number or monogram as on the tunic. Later, grey-green collar patches were adopted by Schützen Regiment 108 with black piping. Officers topcoats such as the Paletot, Überrock, and Mantel remained basically unchanged, the service Paletot with side suspender hooks and cloth tab and button adjustment at the rear cuff.

6. EQUIPMENT (Ausrüstung)

With field dress, pattern '09 ammunition pouches were carried, of natural tan brown leather and worn as three small pouches each side of the belt buckle. All three pouches were stitched to a leather backing which looped over the belt and the centre pouch in each case was provided with a brass buckle to attach to the pack straps. Each pouch contained 20 rounds. Initially the pack, haversack, bivouac sheet and water-bottle remained as in peacetime, but later packs, haversacks and bivouac sheets of field grey canvas material were issued. All leatherware, including belt and pack straps, was left in a natural tan brown condition. The machine-gunners retained their brown leather slings. Entrenching tools were later extended to include picks, hatchets and small wire-cutters, as well as the short-handled spade. Portable saws were also adopted.

7. FIELD CAP (Feldmütze)

Prussia
The field cap of the men remained of the flat visorless pattern, but of grey-green cloth with light green capband and upper crown piping, the Guard Schützen

with a black capband piped light green each side. All cockades were as in peacetime, the imperial above, the state cockade below. The officer's field cap of grey-green cloth or doeskin, with capbands and pipings corresponding in colour to the men's, was of a much softer construction than in peacetime, without side stiffeners and only supported at the centre of the front crown. In addition, the cap possessed a flexible black leather peak and a black leather chinstrap secured each side by a small 1.2cm diameter button and optionally provided with sliding or spiked buckles. All buttons and buckles of blackened brass. The width of the capband did not exceed 4cm, but the diameter of the crown was about 6cm more than the headband and measured vertically across the cockades the cap was officially 10cm high. NCOs with swordknot were permitted the 'extra' officer pattern cap.

Mecklenburg
As Prussia.

Saxony
As Prussia, but with black capband piped light green each side, with black velvet for officers.

Bavaria
As Prussia, but with all cap material of field grey.

COLLAR INSIGNIA

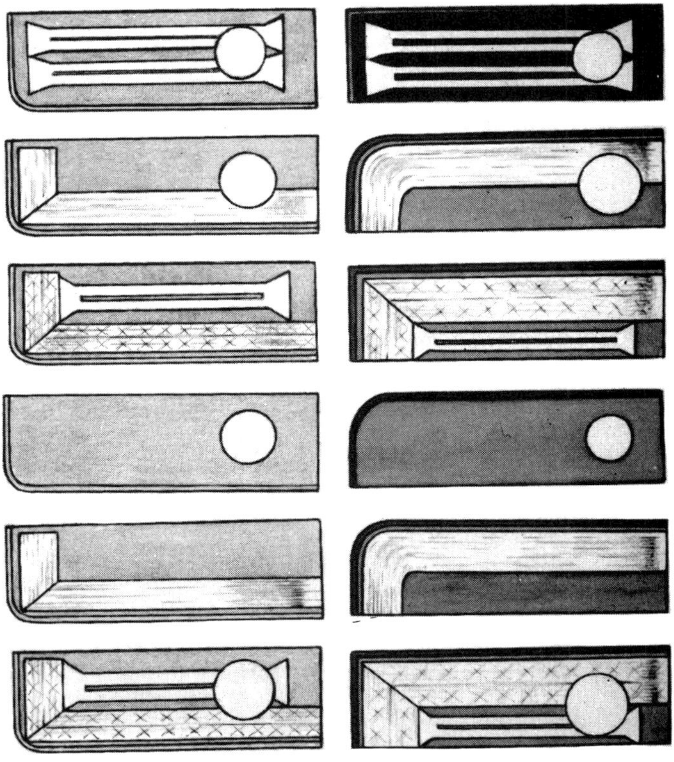

Left hand column:

Grey-green dress—
Gefreiter (Guard);
Sergeant, Vizefeldwebel (Line);
Gefreiter (Line);
Oberjäger (Line);
Sergeant, Vizefeldwebel
Feldwebel (Guard)

Bottom left:

Grey-green dress—
Guard Officer

Right hand column:

Dark green dress—
Gefreiter (Guard Schützen);
Sergeant, Vizefeldwebel,
Feldwebel (Line);
Oberjäger (Guard);
Gefreiter (Line);
Oberjäger (Line);
Sergeant, Vizefeldwebel,
Feldwebel (Guard)

[See Rank List page 3]

CONCLUSION

As the war continued the uniform became increasingly functional with the emphasis placed upon practicability and concealment in the field. By early 1915 modified versions of the field tunic had already appeared and in September 1915 a universal pattern field dress was officially introduced which, to a large extent, though never entirely, replaced the 1910 dress. The field blouse superseded the field tunic and all the more colourful features of the uniform were discarded; the Feldbinde, adjutants' sash, gorget plates, swallows' nests, marksmanship awards and Gibraltar sleeve band were no longer worn in the field, and the whole aspect of the Jäger began to change.

In general service by 1916, the Feldbluse was of a more pronounced shade of grey-green and much looser cut than the earlier field tunic. Fastened, as the Litewka, by a concealed row of grey buttons, the sleeve cuffs were of a deep turn-back pattern without piping or ornament, and on each front skirt a sloping pocket flap, secured by a small tombac crown button, was retained. At the rear the divided skirt was without pocket flaps and only the tombac button-hooks upon the waist seam, together with the side suspender hooks, remained.

The collapsible collar was in a contrasting deeper grey-green 'abzeichen' or badge cloth, and the former golden Oberjäger braid replaced by a dull silver-grey linen band, interwoven on each side with a narrow light green stripe. Later this was abbreviated to only a corner angle on each collar front. The Guard adopted an abbreviated double Kapellen lace, single for the Oberjäger, of silver-grey linen with yellow inner lights, the Guard Jäger with light green centre dart, the Guard Schützen with black. JB14 assumed white inner lights with light green centre stripe. The pointed shoulder straps remained grey-green with red number or monogram, piped light green for the Jäger, and black for the Guard Schützen and Saxon formations.

Guard officers retained their abbreviated matt silver double lace each side of the collar, but no longer upon coloured patches, and now with a dull golden (Mecklenburg silver) upper and lower twisted cord and light green centre light. Shoulder cords remained unaltered, of dull silver flecked with coloured silk and secured by a domed crown button. For both officers and men the universal pattern field trousers now adopted a slate grey tone termed 'Steingrau' with light green seam piping. With these both the black leather marching boots or grey-green puttees with black leather laced ankle boots were worn. Later the so-called 'Stürmhosen' were introduced, with the addition of grey leather knee and seat reinforcement, originally intended only for the specialist Gebirgs and Stürmjäger formations, but becoming generally adopted in the trenches.

An attempt was made, in 1915, to recapture some of the old pre-war colour with the introduction of the grey-green 'peacetime' dress, with coloured pipings and facings, intended for wear in base or home areas, but which never became general issue. Inevitably the grey-green battle-dress became the only uniform, the steel helmet replaced the shako, the wrapped puttees the marching boots, and the old imperial dress was never to return.

Yet whether devised for peace or war the German uniform always retained its peculiarly martial character, the professional touch that revealed not only a pride in but also respect for soldiering. Few uniforms of the time combined so much of their colourful history with the more sombre demands of modern times, and there can be little doubt that all the thoroughness and attention to detail generally attributed to the imperial German Army was equally reflected in its military dress.

SHOULDER STRAP INSIGNIA

from left to right:

Re-enlisted Man (Saxony)

One Year Volunteer (Prussia) with detail of shoulder strap cord

Offizierstellvetreter (Guard)

Offizierstellvetreter (Line)

SHOULDER CORDS

from left to right:

Hauptmann

Leutnant (JB11)

Oberleutnant

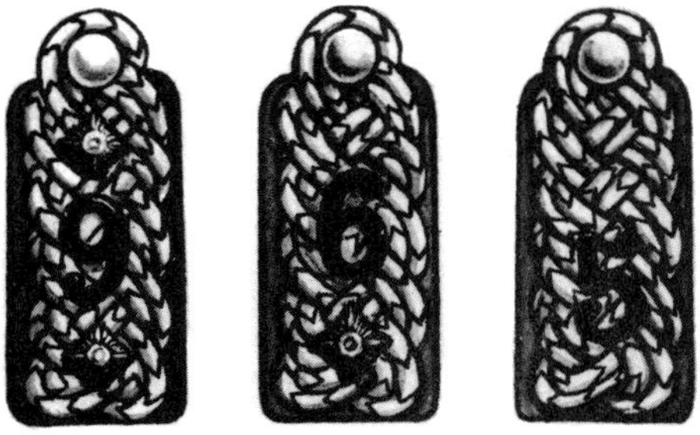

Oberst

Oberstleutnant

Major

APPENDIX A

Orders of Dress (Peacetime 1914)

1. NCOs AND MEN

Parade Dress (Paradeanzug)
Shako with plume. Tunic with full decorations, medals and all marksmanship awards. Long blue/black cloth or white linen trousers. Service belt with attached side-arm, side-arm tassel or swordknot, and ammunition pouches. Pack with strapped mess tin and rolled greatcoat. Rifle carried. Machine-gunners with bandolier sling. NCOs: White leather gloves. During winter months greatcoat worn with cloth trousers inside the marching boots. Church parade on and high festivals without rifle, ammunition pouches or pack, and with long cloth trousers, also when greatcoat worn. Colour-bearers, Music Masters and musicians excused pack.

Guard Dress (Wachtanzug)
Shako. Tunic with full decorations, medals and all marksmanship awards. Service belt with attached side-arm, side-arm tassel or swordknot, and ammunition pouches. Pack with strapped mess tin and rolled greatcoat carried at March-on and March-off. Long blue/black cloth or white linen trousers. Rifle carried. NCOs: White leather gloves. During winter months greatcoat worn with long cloth trousers. On church parade without pack, pouches or rifle.

Orderly Dress (Ordonnanzanzug)
Shako. Tunic with full decorations, medals and marksmanship awards. Service belt with attached side-arm, side-arm tassel or swordknot. Long blue/black cloth or white linen trousers. NCOs: White leather gloves. During winter months greatcoat worn.

Walking-out Dress (Ausgehanzug)
Peaked cap. Tunic with medal ribbon bar only and marksmanship awards. Long blue/black cloth or white linen trousers. Waist belt with attached side-arm, side-arm tassel or swordknot. NCOs: White leather gloves, Men optional. Individual dress effects permitted of black patent leather including service belt. During winter greatcoat worn.

2. OFFICERS

Parade Dress (Paradeanzug)
Shako with plume. Tunic with epaulettes and full orders and decorations. Sword with attached swordknot, body sash or adjutant's sash, and for dis-

mounted officers pack with rolled Paletot. Long blue/black cloth or white linen trousers. Mounted officers cloth breeches inside the high boots, buckled spurs, and parade saddle cloth. White leather gloves. During winter months Paletot worn with breeches inside the high boots, and waist sash. Church parade and high festivals without pack, and with long cloth trousers, also when Paletot worn. Music Masters with shoulder cords and waist girdle.

Service Dress (Dienstanzug)
Shako. Tunic with shoulder cords with full orders and decorations on inspections, church parades, orderly or guard duties, otherwise medal ribbon bar only. Sword with attached swordknot, Feldbinde or adjutant's sash. Long cloth trousers or breeches with high boots. Reddish-brown or white leather gloves. During winter months Paletot worn with Feldbinde. Music Masters with waist girdle.

Undress (Kleiner Dienstanzug)
Peaked cap or shako. Tunic, Überrock or Litewka with shoulder cords. Sword with swordknot. Long blue/black cloth or white linen trousers, on more informal or field occasions also breeches with high boots. Reddish-brown or white leather gloves. During winter months Paletot worn.

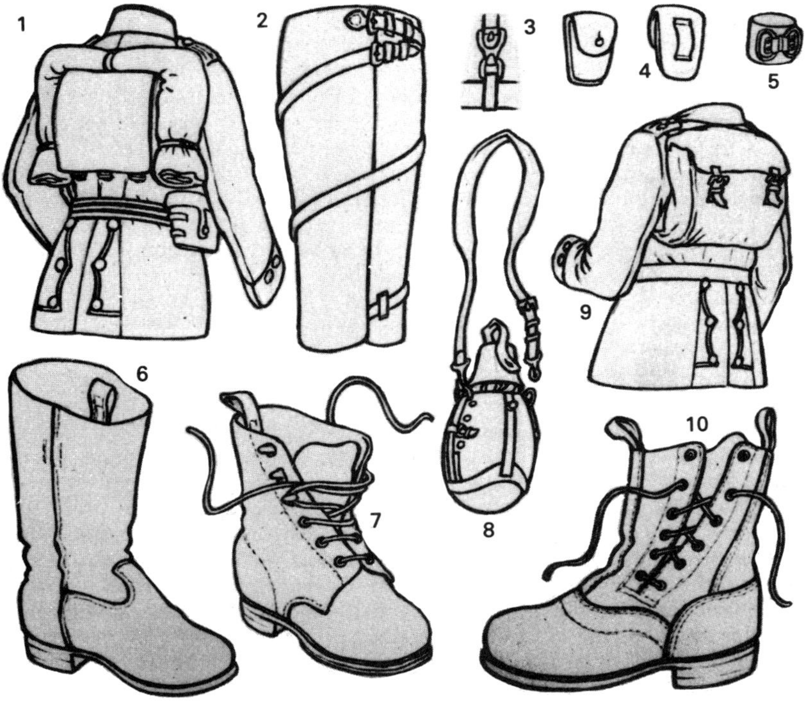

1. Officer's Pack, black leather
2. M.G. Company Gaiters
3. Brace Attachment and Belt Loop
4. M.G. Company Ammunition Pouches
5. Metal Cup with folding Handles
6. Marching Boot or Jack Boot
7. Front Laced Boot 1901 Pattern
8. Medical Personnel Water Bottle
9. Jäger Cycle Company Rucksack
10. Side-laced Boot, 1893 Pattern

APPENDIX B

Medals and Decorations

On parade or ceremonial the 'Grosse Ordensschnalle' or full orders and decorations, together with ribbons, was worn. The sash of an order, unless otherwise stipulated, was worn from the left shoulder to the right hip, passing under the epaulette and beneath the waist sash, normally displaying at its lower end both the star and grand cross of the order. Only a single sash was displayed at any one time, with membership of further orders indicated by additional neck crosses or breast stars. The grand cross was suspended at the neck from a broad ribbon, the star of an order pinned to the centre of the left breast and any additional crosses or stars were placed beneath in a correspondingly lower position. The grand cross, and in some cases the first class of an order, conferred the status of Grand Commander and was generally confined to royal Cols-in-Chief and Generals of noble or very high rank.

Neck orders, in a slightly reduced form of the grand cross, generally corresponding to a second or third class of the order, carried the status of Knight Commander and were generally awarded to the lower ranking Generals and staff officers, but in wartime for exceptional bravery in the field were often extended to the subalterns, as for example the Order Pour le Mérite. As the grand cross, the commander cross was suspended from a ribbon, though somewhat narrower, the highest state award assuming the uppermost position, with additional orders placed beneath in order of precedence. A Saxon officer for example would display the Military Order of St Henry above the Prussian Pour le Mérite and vice versa.

The knight's cross or lower grades of an order, together with all further decorations and medals, were displayed on the left upper tunic breast in strict order of seniority from the wearer's right to left. The ribbons were displayed in the draped or trapezoid manner favoured by many central European countries, with the base of the ribbons roughly in line with the second front tunic-buttonhole. In broad terms the ribbon row commenced with the highest orders of the particular state, followed by those of the allied German states, then the non-German European states, and finally those of the non-European or foreign states. In practice there were exceptions to this, certain orders being given preferential display, and for all states the Iron Cross, if awarded, normally assumed precedence. Furthermore, in the case of Prussia, if awarded for military services, the Order of the Red Eagle, the Order of the Crown, and the House Order of Hohenzollern were carried on a campaign ribbon, in effect black with white edging stripes as for the Iron Cross, instead of the statutory ribbon. Pin-back decorations without ribbons were also displayed on the left lower breast with, under certain circumstances, the ribbon only of a knight's cross or campaign decoration passed diagonally through the second front buttonhole. Jubilee or commemorative clasps were also permitted on the left upper breast beneath the ribbon row.

On undress or walking out occasions the 'Kleine Ordensschnalle' or ribbons only was displayed on the left upper breast, and decorations were confined to a minimum upon the tunic, Litewka or Überrock, generally restricted to a neck order, a pin-back breast decoration, a ribbon passed through the second front button hole, and a commemorative clasp. The Order Pour le Mérite, The Iron Cross 1st Class, or Jerusalem Cross, if possessed, were always displayed. If a crown or crossed swords was associated with the decoration this was mounted in miniature form upon the ribbon. As a rule, decorations were not worn upon the Paletot, but officers so distinguished were permitted on parade or ceremonial to wear an order sash from the left shoulder to the right hip, and to display a neck order, in reality suspended from the tunic collar, but otherwise nothing. Normally only the suspension ring of a neck order was revealed at the collar.

CUFFS

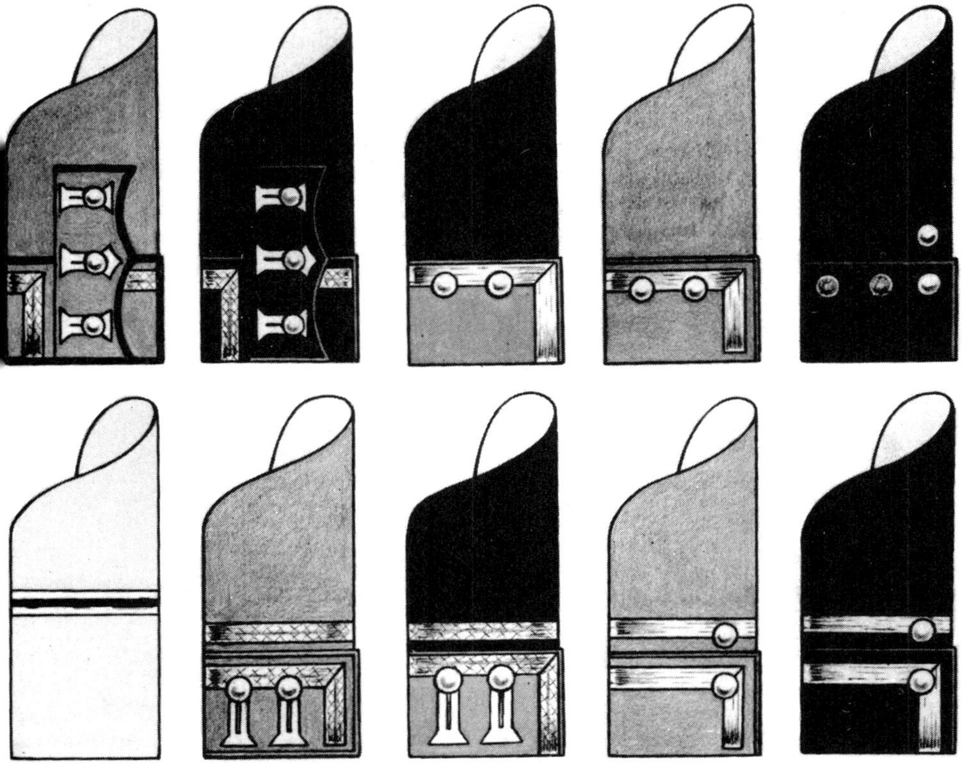

Top row left to right:

Oberjäger (Guard Schützen)—Grey-green dress, Dark green dress; Oberjäger (Line)—Dark-green dress, Grey-green dress; Marksmanship School (Saxony)—Dark green dress.

Bottom row left to right:

Feldwebel—Drill tunic; Feldwebel (Guard Jäger)—Grey-green dress, Dark green dress; Feldwebel (Saxony)—Grey-green dress, Dark green dress.

[See Rank List page 3.]

APPENDIX C

The Jäger & Schützen
(Peacetime 1914)

Royal Prussian Guard Jäger Btn	Raised 15.6.1744. Garrisoned Potsdam. Guard Corps.
Royal Prussian Guard Schützen Btn	Raised 19.5.1814. Garrisoned Berlin/ Lichterfelde. Guard Corps.
Royal Prussian Jäger Btn Count York v Wartenburg (East Prussian) No 1	Raised 15.6.1744. Garrisoned Ortelsburg. Army Corps XX.
Royal Prussian Jäger Btn Prince Bismarck (Pomeranian) No 2	Raised 15.6.1744. Garrisoned Kulm. Army Corps XVII.
Royal Prussian Brandenburg Jäger Btn No 3	Raised 21.6.1815. Garrisoned Lübben. Army Corps III.
Royal Prussian Magdeburg Jäger Btn No 4	Raised 21.6.1815. Garrisoned Naumburg/ Saale. Army Corps IV.
Royal Prussian Jäger Btn v Neumann (1st Silesian) No 5	Raised 21.11.1808. Garrisoned Hirschberg. Army Corps V.
Royal Prussian 2nd Silesian Jäger Btn No 6	Raised 21.11.1808. Garrisoned Oels Army Corps VI.
Royal Prussian Westphalian Jäger Btn No 7	Raised 3.10.1815. Garrisoned Bückeburg. Army Corps VII.
Royal Prussian Rhenish Jäger Btn No 8	Raised 3.10.1815. Garrisoned Schlettstadt. Army Corps XV.
Royal Prussian Lauenburg Jäger Btn No 9	Raised 21.6.1866. Garrisoned Ratzeburg. Army Corps IX.
Royal Prussian Hanoverian Jäger Btn No 10	Raised 19.12.1803. Garrisoned Goslar/ Harz. Army Corps X.
Royal Prussian Electorate of Hesse Jäger Btn No 11	First raised 1631, re-raised 5.12.1813 Garrisoned Marburg. Army Corps XI.
Royal Saxon 1st Jäger Btn No 12	Raised 1.11.1809. Garrisoned Freiberg XII. (1st Royal Saxon) Army Corps.
Royal Saxon 2nd Jäger Btn No 13	Raised 31.8.1809. Garrisoned Dresden XII. (1st Royal Saxon) Army Corps.
Grand-ducal Mecklenburg Jäger Btn No 14	Raised 1.6.1821. Garrisoned Colmar XV. Army Corps.
Royal Saxon Schützen (Fusilier) Regt 'Prince George' No 108	Raised 1.10.1809. Garrisoned Dresden XII. (1st Royal Saxon) Army Corps.
Royal Bavarian 1st Jäger Btn	Raised 27.11.1815. Garrisoned Freising. 1st Royal Bav Army Corps.
Royal Bavarian 2nd Jäger Btn	Raised 1.12.1825. Garrisoned Aschaffenburg. 2nd Royal Bav Army Corps.

Padded Dress for Bayonet Training and Fatigue Dress 1913 (Jäger—Prussia)

Signaller's Sleeve Badge

Medical Personnel Sleeve Badge

Feldwebel Litewka Chevron (Guard)

Bibliography

Jany, C.: *Geschichte der Preussischen Armee,* Biblio-Verlag, Osnabrück, 1967.

Jürgens, H.: *Friedensuniformen des deutschen Heeres 1914.* 1. Infanterie. H.G. Schulz, Hamburg, 1954.

Knotel-sieg: *Handbuch für Uniformkunde,* H.G. Schülz, Hamburg, 1937.

Mila, A.: *Geschichte der Bekleidung und Ausrüstung der Königlich Preussischen Armee 1808–1878,* E.S. Mittler & Sohn, Berlin, 1878.

Pietsch, P.: *Formations und Uniformierungseschichte des Preussischen Heeres 1808–1914, Band I Fusstruppen.* H.G. Schulz, Hamburg, 1963/66.

Transfeldt-v Brand-Quenstedt: *Wort und Brauch im deutschen Heer,* H.G. Schulz, Hamburg, 1967.

Ski-Jager, 1914 (Württemberg)